Driven to Win

DRIVEN TO WIN

AN AUTOBIOGRAPHY

Nigel Mansell
and Derick Allsop

ARROW BOOKS

Arrow Books Limited
62–65 Chandos Place, London WC2N 4NW

An imprint of Century Hutchinson Limited

London Melbourne Sydney Auckland
Johannesburg and agencies throughout
the world

First published 1988 by Stanley Paul

Arrow edition 1989

Phototypeset by Input Typesetting Ltd, London
Printed and bound in Great Britain by
Courier International Ltd, Tiptree, Essex

ISBN 0 09 963440 6

Contents

To Rosanne,
for giving me the strength
to make my crazy dreams come true,
and to the memory of my mother
and Colin.

Acknowledgements

The compilation of this book owes so much to so many. We would like to thank, in particular: Sue Allsop, Ann Bradshaw, Nick Brittan, Canon, Peter Collins, Peter Dyke, Maurice Hamilton, the Manx Museum and National Trust, Sue Membery, Patrick Mulleady, Oulton Park, Stuart Sykes, Peter Windsor and Byron Young.

Thanks are also due to the following for allowing the use of copyright photographs: Action Images, AllSport/Dan Smith, AllSport/Pascal Rondeau, Lawrence Levy, Mark Newcombe, Nigel Snowdon, Sporting Pictures, Keith Sutton and John Townsend.

Foreword

From the day the seeds of this book were sown, Nigel Mansell was insistent that it would tell the true, complete story of his life and his racing career. To that end he has been frank in his opinions, revealing about his previously unknown past and responsive to the most searching, even painful questioning. A two-minute silence on my tape captures the anguish of a man attempting to put into words his recollections of the day his former team-mate, Elio de Angelis, was fatally injured.

I do not put into Nigel's mouth words that patently should not be his. I have therefore followed a format that enables me to qualify and to quantify. Nigel has his say, I have mine. Others, notably Nigel's wife Rosanne, and Peter Collins, ex-Lotus official and now team boss of Benetton, assist the colouring of the pages. Rosanne, as candid as her husband, gives her own views on Nigel, their relationship and their common ambition. Her contribution to this book is as essential as the one she has given to Nigel's career.

Derick Allsop

1

Driving On

A grey, forbidding afternoon at Rio de Janeiro. Friday's hot sunshine, which pushed the temperature up to 104 degrees, gave way to destructive overnight storms and now dark uncertainty shrouds the circuit. So little this weekend seems sure. A new Formula One Championship beckons, complete with new regulations, new hopes, new fears. There are more restrictions on the turbos in this, their final year. Will the normally aspirated contenders return to the front line? Or must they still succumb to raw power?

All winter there have been nagging questions, too, about the driver in car No 5. Has he fully recovered from that crash in Japan, more than five months past? Can he in this, his first competitive drive since, expect to recapture his form of the previous two, dazzling years? He no longer has the most feared machine on the track, so how can he compete? Does he even have the nerve or the will to compete again?

Qualifying for the first race of 1988, the Brazilian Grand Prix, is into its closing stages as car No 5, a Canon Williams, powered by a normally aspirated Judd engine, winds up for a flying lap. The pit crew watch the car as it screams along the straight, until it disappears round the corner. Elsewhere, eyes are on the Olivetti Longines screens, which instantly update times and grid positions. Surely no one will prevent Marlboro McLaren, now with the muscle of Honda turbos, from occupying both places on the front row. Not the Williams, anyway. It is 14 mph slower down the straight.

Car No 5 takes the last corner, a seemingly never-ending right-hander, eventually straightens and lunges for the line. Up come the figures – 1:28.632. Depending on allegiance, emotions range from delight to despair. But up and down the pit lane there is a common reaction, one of utter admiration. The time of 1 minute 28.632 seconds is stunning. It is too good for Alain Prost's McLaren. Only Ayrton Senna's McLaren can beat it. No other normally aspirated challenger can make the first three rows.

The driver of car No 5 climbs from his cockpit, removes his gloves and helmet, peels off his balaclava and delivers his verdict.

That was one of the best laps of my career. I'm amazed to be on the front row. I had to be right on the limit to get that time.

The driver of car No 5 is Nigel Mansell. And he's back in business.

Nigel had crashed during qualifying for the Japanese Grand Prix on 30 October 1987. It was an agonising final act of a title drama that gripped the public and left him runner-up in the Championship for the second successive year. In 1986 he was all but there. Then a tyre exploded, taking his dreams with it, just 44 miles short of the line at Adelaide, Australia. This time his quest was over two races from the end. He was flown home with a back injury. If he were to continue racing, the repair work – psychological as well as physical would have to start immediately.

I'd had a few accidents in my career but I'd never suffered the pain I suffered after that shunt at Suzuka. I was brought back to my home, on the Isle of Man, that weekend. Over the following few days I had a number of specialist examinations and X-rays. I was found to have what the specialist described as spinal concussion. All the vertebrae in my back were concussed and one of them was actually crushed.

To complicate matters I also had a couple of fractured ribs, which didn't show up on the X-rays until some weeks later. That explained not only the more general discomfort but also the breathing problems I'd been having. I found talking for any period of time a big effort – and a painful one at that. I was gasping for breath.

Right from those first few days the specialist told me that the damage would take time to heal up. I was told I had to be patient, to rest and give it time. He was right. For two months I could do very little. That was bad enough. But it seemed to me I wasn't really getting much better. Not at the rate I would have liked, anyway. It was very hard to take.

I had a lot of time to think, to take stock. I had time to talk to my wife Rosanne, time to be with our children, even if I couldn't play with them. Chloe was five, Leo not yet three. Just a week after I came back from Japan our third child, Greg Nigel, was born. Having a family around me gave me a lot of comfort, but it's not easy when your five-year-old daughter tells you she doesn't want you to race and get hurt again. You try to explain that it's your job, that it has to be done. You say you won't get hurt again, but you know there is no way you can promise that.

Throughout my career Rosanne has shared everything with me, the good times and the bad. I knew what she was going through at that time. She suffered with me, just as she had suffered with me before. It is so difficult for a wife, so very difficult.

But when we discussed things we realised there was so much to be positive about. If I'd had a bad year I might have taken a negative view, but I hadn't. Far from it. I'd had a fantastic year. In fact, I'd had two fantastic years. Over that two-year period, starting in late 1985, I'd won thirteen races. In the 1986 season I had five victories; in 1987 six victories. No one else had more than three wins in 1987. Given reasonable luck I would perhaps have had three or even four more wins. I'd been consistently fast in qualifying, beating a record of thirty-four years' standing with my fifteenth consecutive place on the front row of the grid. I reckoned that all added up to something to be proud of.

All this was something to build on and progress from, not throw away. When you think things through like that the pain doesn't really become a factor in the decision-making. You want to get well again, and as soon as possible. But it's not in my character to give up and retire in such a situation. I want to fight back, to get out in that car again just as quickly as I can. The mental battle was always going to be won. I was definitely going to carry on racing.

Nelson Piquet, newly crowned champion, was switching from Williams to Lotus for 1988 so Mansell would have a new partner, Italian Riccardo Patrese, and new status in the team – No 1.

Too much is made of this No 1/No 2 driver business. As I'd proved over the previous two years, it didn't really matter whether I was No 1 or No 2. The three Williams cars had been identical and, as we'd demonstrated, all were capable of winning races. Nevertheless, it was satisfying to have that position for the first time in my career and with it the extra car to work with. You are not so likely to be kept inactive by breakdowns.

New also for 1988 was the engine. Honda's power, efficiency and reliability had accompanied Williams back to the top, but now the massive Japanese organisation had decided it was time for a change. They formed an alliance with McLaren, although they retained their association with Lotus. Williams turned to John Judd,

*a benign Englishman who built normally aspirated
engines at a modest factory on the outskirts of Rugby.*

Williams and Honda made a tremendous combination.
When you get two concerns like those together, pooling
their expertise and resources, you are going to come up
with Championships. In those years I don't think
Honda could have won it without Williams. They were
still learning, still developing. Now they're with
McLaren and the ball is rolling.

Things were obviously going to be different. We
wouldn't have the power of the turbos and we wouldn't
have the squads of engine men pouring all over the car.
But John Judd had a good reputation in the sport and
we believed that more power would come with development work. What we really wanted was reliability. If
you don't finish, you don't score points.

Yes, there was still a lot to be optimistic about. You
don't go on unless you have that optimism, that belief.
I am motivated now the way I have always been motivated – by the will to be successful. I have been successful
in the past and I feel I can be successful in the future.
While I feel like this, retirement won't be a consideration. I want to go on for several more years.

To a certain extent, though, that could be out of my
hands, because essentially this business, like so many
others, is about supply and demand. If there remains a
demand for me, great. If the demand isn't there and
people don't wish to pay the going rate, then maybe
that's the time to pack it in.

But then, the financial consideration is secondary
anyway. You have to WANT to do this, and want
it passionately. The rewards of Formula One can be
considerable and I have reached a stage when I could
retire and live comfortably. Yet still I have this love of
driving, of competing, of trying to win. No amount of

money can buy that. You either enjoy it, or you get out.

I had no doubts about my ability to go on. Certain people would say that I don't have any natural talent and that all I've achieved has been through sheer hard work. But a racing driver doesn't maintain a consistent pace and win races regularly simply through hard work. He has to have a certain degree of natural ability, then work on it and refine it. I've never met the complete, natural driver. But without that natural base, you'll never create a winner no matter how much hard work you put into it.

Throughout my career I have had to put up with the doubters, but now I have nothing to prove. My record speaks for itself. Having had so many traumatic experiences and setbacks in my career I would say I have become a more mature, more complete person. I can cope with people who try to hurt me or my family. I have a much greater understanding of life and people. That's why I have chosen to write this book now.

During those winter months of 1987/8 I mapped out the coming year very carefully. I would prepare thoroughly for the season and I would use my time to maximum effect. After two months of doing nothing I began running and exercising again. But I'd put on weight and had to do something drastic. I went to a health clinic in Austria.

I was there for four days and it seemed like forever. I was training hard all day – running, swimming, riding mountain bikes – and eating almost nothing. A bit of rabbit food, that was about it. It was hell, like a concentration camp. All the time I was there I was hungry, and when I got back home I was still hungry because I was on a diet. But it had to be done. To do this job well and do it safely you have to be fit.

A fortnight later he was cleared by a specialist to resume

*driving. Even then, however, he was by no means fully
recovered. He was accompanied on the trip to Jerez,
Spain, for his first test drive since the crash, by a registered osteopath experienced in the treatment of rally
drivers. It was his opinion that Mansell's back needed
'sorting out', but there was no time for that now. He
could only hope to soothe and ease the inevitable pain.
At 10.21 a.m. on Monday 15 February, 108 days after
his accident, Mansell was back on a race track.*

The first test was very difficult. The car was probably
being kind to me, because it kept breaking down. We
were there four days and didn't get anything like the
mileage we intended. One morning it took me the best
part of an hour to get out of bed and dressed. I had
aches and pains and felt dreadfully stiff. It was quite
distressing. I was supposed to be driving again that
morning, but I was in a terrible state. Once I was up
and moving about, though, I loosened up and managed
to drive.

I knew it wasn't going to be easy. I couldn't expect
it to be. Driving a Grand Prix car is nothing like driving
a road car. The speeds, particularly the cornering speeds
with all the G-loading, demand particular strengths. It's
tough enough in one of those things when you are fully
fit, let alone when you are recovering from injury. But
for me the best possible route to fitness was in the car,
and if it was an ordeal then it was an ordeal I had to
put up with.

Besides, there were good points to come out of the
test. While we didn't cover the ground we'd planned,
our interim car was quick and I put in a few good times.
What's more, I found I still liked that certain feeling
you get at the wheel of a Formula One car. For all the
aches and pains, it was good to be back at the job
again. The new car, the car we would be using in the
1988 Championship, would soon be ready. Then we

could get down to work. The winter had been long
enough.

*Testing in Rio was again a mixed bag. There were
problems, which meant long, boring delays, and there
were bursts of activity which suggested the potential
was there. The next trip to Rio would be for the real
thing. Mansell arrived in Brazil the morning of Wednesday 30 March – minus moustache.*

I'd been going on at the team and John Judd about
needing more power and they came back at me saying
I needed to lose some weight. So I shaved off the moustache and said: 'Right, I've got rid of some weight,
now give me some more power!' I'd had a moustache
for more than seventeen years, but I thought maybe it
was time for a change, that perhaps it might bring me
a change of luck. Either way, I was quite happy with
the result; so was Rosanne, and most people seemed to
think it suited me.

In a number of respects I anticipated things being
different in 1988. I couldn't expect to be the front
runner, but it seemed to me that that might be quite
pleasant. The pressure would be off me and on others.
But there would be some circuits, the slower ones,
where we might reasonably expect some success. The
plan was to make the most of those opportunities and
pick up what we could on the quicker circuits.

Whether normally aspirated engines are safer is
doubtful. They don't have the straight-line speed; but I
was amazed to find that they were faster through the
corners.

I'd come to terms with the situation in my own mind
and saw everything so clearly. I had a fresh perspective
on the whole business. The quality of my machinery
would decide how much I could achieve. I would do
my best for myself, my team and my country, but I
could do no more than that. My attitude was very

relaxed, even laid-back about the whole thing. I've educated myself to be a realist. If the car develops problems, there's nothing I can do about it and no point getting upset. Nothing can change things. What has happened is history. All you can hope for is the chance to fight another day.

Physically I felt pretty good. I wasn't at the peak of fitness, but then it didn't make sense to overdo the training in the weeks leading up to the first race and so drain or even injure myself. I'm sure it would have been a mistake to rush my fitness. In a hot country like Brazil you need all the strength and stamina you can muster. What I needed was driving.

When the drivers turned up for first practice on Friday 1 April, the leading contender for April Fool was Nelson Piquet. His rivalry with Mansell had deteriorated from merely unfriendly to openly hostile. Now, reported extracts of an article in the Brazilian edition of Playboy *magazine served to refuel the conflict. Piquet was quoted as calling Mansell an 'uneducated blockhead'. Not content with that, he made an insulting personal attack on Rosanne.*

Hard-bitten drivers were appalled and angry. Piquet had not only offended the Mansells but demeaned his status as champion of their sport. Britain's Derek Warwick voiced their disapproval: 'Families are off limits. The sooner Piquet gets out of Formula One the better.' Mansell conducted himself with remarkable restraint.

As far as I'm concerned the guy just doesn't exist. What he said about my wife is quite incredible, but I don't really have to say any more because that would be lowering myself to his standards. Everyone else can judge and see him for what he is. I merely made sure the Lotus team were advised it would be wise for him to keep out of my way and not stray down to our pit! That was the first weekend I'd worked with Riccardo

Patrese, and it made a pleasant change to have a team-mate I could actually communicate with. It was a one thousand per cent improvement.

If anyone thought the 'laid-back' Mansell would be less than committed out on the track, he soon delivered absolute proof that as far as his driving was concerned, nothing had changed. Once strapped into his car, the adrenalin coursing, the challenge inviting, he was as quick and decisive as ever.

The timetable for a Grand Prix weekend follows a familiar pattern – Friday and Saturday 10 to 11.30 a.m. practice; 1 to 2 p.m. qualifying. On Sunday the race time varies, usually according to the demands of television. At the end of the first qualifying session Mansell was second on the grid behind Senna. That was commendable enough. But to retain his position at the end of the second day, when the turbos had flexed their muscles and found their stride, was astonishing.

The Brazilian Grand Prix was scheduled to launch the 1988 Formula One Championship at 1 p.m. local time, but as Senna, sitting on the grid, selected first, the gear linkage broke. He waved his arms and the start was aborted. Senna switched cars and had to start from the pit lane – only to be later disqualified for changing after the green flag – which left Mansell effectively on pole.

Alain Prost led into the first corner, though. I couldn't match the McLaren's power. Then Gerhard Berger went through to take second place in the Ferrari. I settled down in third place and I was quite satisfied with the way it was going. It began to look better still when I started to pull in Gerhard. I got to within a second of him, but as I did so the temperatures shot up. The engine was overheating, so I went into the pits to see what we could do. But there the engine stalled and just wouldn't fire up again: throttle . . . nothing. After several minutes we had to give up. There was nothing else we could do.

It was a big disappointment because it looked as though we were on for second place, and that would have been a hell of a start for us. But you have to finish, and we managed only eighteen laps. The mechanics later discovered the reason we couldn't get away again – a broken ignition wire. That's motor racing for you.

But there was still a lot from the weekend to encourage us, and we'd learned one or two things. That race was gone; all that mattered was the next one.

The next one took him to Imola, in Italy, for the San Marino Grand Prix, and provided sobering confirmation of the challenge ahead.

I'd been on the front row and won the race the year before, and we hoped the turbos would have problems with only 150 litres of fuel on what is a very thirsty track. For a start, though, qualifying didn't go well. After sixteen consecutive front-row places, I was eleventh! I just couldn't make the car go any quicker. I knew I was going to have to face that situation some day so there was no point getting upset about it. We had work to do.

Riccardo was sixth and clearly his car was working better than mine. Fortunately we now had a situation where we were working together as a team and the information was being shared. We made one or two changes to the reactive suspension and aerodynamics. We found a bit more on the Sunday morning warm-up and, sure enough, it was different again. I was third fastest behind the two McLarens.

A shower of rain about half an hour before the race did nothing for my confidence, but the clouds passed and we switched back to slicks for the start. My concern then was the danger of overheating. We had new oil pumps to ease the problem caused by centrifugal cornering forces, but I knew I would still have to pace myself, drive in a controlled, disciplined manner and time my strikes just right. I couldn't afford to get stuck close behind anyone for too long.

I was tenth after the first lap, sat and watched the race settle, then began to make my move. The McLarens were already away in their own world. Senna led from pole position to the flag. Prost didn't get off well but was up to second on the eighth lap, and by the end the pair of them had lapped the rest. In our race I took Berger for seventh place and came up behind the Benettons and my team-mate. As Riccardo dropped back I went to sixth and had to put two wheels on the grass to take Thierry Boutsen for fifth. When Alessandro Nannini had a spin I slipped through to fourth place.

That was lap thirty-six. There were twenty-four laps left and one man stood between me and a place on the podium. That man was Piquet. I tracked him for four laps, picked my moment and darted by. That was very satisfying, both professionally and personally. On the next lap he turned up the boost and there was nothing I could do to stop him. Even with a 2.5 bar boost limit on a fuel circuit like Imola, the Honda turbos had far too much for us.

I didn't have a chance to make another attack. On lap forty-three an electrical fault caused the engine to quit and that, in turn, crippled the suspension. All I could do was coast back to the pits. It was sickening to have driven so well in Rio and at Imola and yet have nothing to show for it. The situation was difficult for the team and for me – perhaps the toughest of my career, in fact. After being out in front with a winning car for two and a half years, I had to live with this period of struggle. We weren't finishing races, so we were in trouble. Simple as that. But it wasn't a time to drop our heads and give in. We had to be positive and we had to fight. We had made some progress and would work in that direction. It was another mountain to climb – and we were going to tackle it.

Even at Monaco it was impossible for us to compete with the turbos. I've never had so many hairy moments as I had there in the 1988 qualifying sessions. I was kissing the barriers, going straight on. I really scared myself. But after four years on the front row I couldn't manage better than fifth behind the McLarens and the Ferraris. At least I was the fastest of the aspirated runners.

We had made some progress with the cooling problem, though it was still a big concern. I couldn't afford to get caught up in traffic for too long, yet at Monaco you can hardly avoid it. I spent the early part of the race holding my ground in fourth place. I gradually moved up behind Prost – who eventually won when Senna crashed – but it was a hell of a job trying to hang on to those turbos. I simply couldn't keep up.

So then I concentrated on maintaining what I had. Michele Alboreto tracked me in the Ferrari but I was able to cope with that – until he suddenly dived inside me at the swimming pool. I came in on my line and he spun me into the barrier. There was nothing I could do. I was out of the race again and he went on to take third place.

The stewards called us after the race but Michele apologised and I accepted that. They saw that our attitude was very professional and had no cause to take the matter any further. Michele isn't the sort of driver to shunt you off deliberately and, disappointed though I was, I didn't make a fuss about it. You simply put it down to racing and get on with it. Tomorrow is another day – and it's always tomorrow that matters.

2

Growing Pains

Upton-on-Severn, Worcestershire, England. A gentle, unhurried, unassuming corner of the world. Life, like the river, passes through with scarcely a backward glance. Nigel Ernest James Mansell was born here on 8 August 1953, the third of four children to Eric and Joyce Mansell – soon, like the waters of the Severn, to move on and seek his own course.

My parents ran a tea-room where they also lived, and I was born in one of the upstairs rooms there. We moved around quite a lot when I was young. I was three or four when we left Upton and went to the Midlands. We seemed to have so many family houses. The first house I recall was in Hall Green, south of Birmingham, where we stayed for a few years. All the moving also meant changing schools. I attended about four schools and four different technical colleges after that. I did reasonably well at school, finishing up with a couple of O levels and quite a few CSEs. But it didn't make it any easier switching schools so many times.

The thing I enjoyed most about my first two schools was being captain of the football and cricket teams. I always loved sport and games. At my second school, Wellsbourne, I worked my way into the chess team deliberately to get out of Latin. I just hated Latin. In fact, I wasn't too interested in the academic side at all until I moved to Hall Green Bilateral.

Even then, though, it was a rather traumatic experience. Wellsbourne had closed down and I didn't start with the normal intake. I joined in the middle of the year and was virtually on my own. Previously, I'd always been in classes of about fifteen; suddenly it was thirty. I'd always been to all-boys schools; now it was mixed. I had no friends there, and I got into trouble and fights. It was a difficult time, but I started to learn how to look after myself.

It didn't help when I had to take time off school to go karting. The school was fine about it, but some of the kids weren't. When I was picked to represent the country in Holland, the headmaster was genuinely pleased for me and announced at assembly that I was getting a special two-week leave. Afterwards in the playground I got a cricket bat across my legs and was beaten up somewhat. They were presumably a bit jealous and thought it was favouritism. The truth is that getting time off doesn't help anyone, because you have to work harder to catch up on your school work. That's not an easy situation for an eleven-year-old.

Tougher times still lay ahead. Master Mansell had already developed a passion for motors and movement. He talked of becoming a racing driver, but then he talked of many things. A young boy's head is full of dreams.

At a young age you are very impressionable, and there's no doubt that watching the late Jimmy Clark drive inspired me. But it wouldn't be accurate to say that one particular thing sparked me off. Like any other child I wanted to be an astronaut, or a policeman, or an RAF jet fighter pilot, or a fire-engine driver . . . or a racing driver. We had a helper in the house called Mrs Harris. A lovely lady. I was very close to her. I remember following her round when I was young. She has said that I told her I was going to do all those other things. I suppose the interesting point is that they all have an element of danger. My involvement in motor racing was a natural progression.

I learnt to drive on a farm at Whythall. It was owned by the parents of one of my Wellsbourne school-mates, Michael Webster, whom I haven't seen or spoken to for years. We were about ten and used to drive a battered old Austin Seven around the farm land. We had some fantastic adventures, driving this thing through fields with such long grass you couldn't see further than the bonnet. I suppose we were doing only about 10 or 15 mph, but it was exhilarating, all right. We had a few spills, of course, but it was just good fun. I didn't think at that time that I had any particular driving skills. It was just something we did.

My father raced karts a bit in the Midlands. He later told me that I had got my courage from him. My feeling is that courage comes from within oneself. I remember, though, that he was very bitter because I said I got my speed from my mother. I was much closer to my mother than to my father, and I think he was jealous. I believe I've got my mother to thank for a great deal of what I've achieved. She was an incredibly quick driver on the road, much faster than my father. One hundred mph, 110 mph – it was nothing to my mother, and she drove anything. She was a crazy lady. Wonderful, but on the road, crazy. On one occasion when I was young she even spun me in the snow in an Austin 1100. She got in a rut and we just went spinning round and round in the middle of the road.

I was also encouraged by my brother-in-law. He was very excited about the prospect of getting a go-kart, or racing kart as they are called now. We bought our first kart for £25, which included a lawn-mower engine. We had some great times. You can imagine what it meant to a lad of nine or ten. The only problem was that the kart was driven by just one wheel rather than two, so it would go round left-hand corners quickly but on right-hand corners come almost to a stop. Anywhere clockwise and you were in trouble.

We used a path round the allotments as a track and inevitably had a few mishaps, although nothing too serious. We didn't go fast. All that mattered was the enjoyment. I suppose the appeal was the simple fact that a kart could propel you without pedalling. I could beat anyone round those allotments, so I suppose it was the obvious next step to go into competition. You had to be eleven to get a licence, so there were a few of us aged nine or ten telling people we were eleven so that we could race. Up through the classes in racing a lot of lads lied about their ages because they couldn't wait to get out on to the track. On the other hand, when I was around twenty-six, I seemed to get stuck there for an extra year and I didn't argue when people kept saying I was twenty-six instead of twenty-seven.

I was ten when I had my first competitive race. It was at Shennington, Edge Hill, Banbury. There we were, with our one-wheel drive Fastakart with a JLO engine, and I thought 'Right, I'm going to win my first race.' It was an incredible eye-opener for me. In practice before the heats I was going up the straight and all of a sudden the engine stopped. I pulled over to the side and a flag marshal ran over to me and asked me if I was all right. I said I was and that it was only the chain that had come off. He said: 'Your chain's come off? Your bloody engine's come off!' I looked back and, sure enough, no engine. All the engine mounts were so old that they'd fallen off. So there behind me down the straight, lay the engine, the exhaust pipe and everything else.

Even when we got the engine welded back on we were so uncompetitive that the others were doing two laps to my one, and a lap was only half a mile. Other boys there were anything up to sixteen, so I was very much the baby, and very upset at the time. I had tears in my eyes. Round the allotment I could beat my brother-in-law, my father, my friends, everybody, so I thought we could go racing with what we had. But when I got to a proper race I found myself up against all these karts – hybrids really, with drives on both wheels, different sprocket sizes for different circuits and different straights. There we were with a fixed small sprocket, so basic it was ridiculous. We didn't know anything about minimum weights; our kart was 40lb overweight, and we had only a 100cc engine. At that age I didn't understand anything about tuning or how to get more power. I just couldn't believe all those people were beating me so easily. I was down at the time, but it just pushed us on to get a faster kart, a new kart and a newer engine.

A brand-new engine then cost about £30; now a new engine on those lines would cost around £500. Karting has gone barmy. In those days if you had any problems you could go and borrow an engine from a neighbour. If you didn't have a bit of equipment, someone would either give it to you or lend it to you. There might be a hundred competitors, and everybody knew everybody else. If there was an accident everyone was most concerned. The competition on the track was fierce, but there was a feeling of comradeship. If anyone was naughty he was stamped on, especially in the younger classes.

Instead of doing my homework in the evening – which I now make my children do – I used to go home and work on my kart, tuning the engine, fiddling about, polishing it up. If I had polished it one night I would still go home the next night and polish it again. It was a fascination for me, and one I certainly don't regret. It kept me off the streets, and we started winning races.

We were a very close family at that time, but not a wealthy family. My grandparents used to help out – they bought me one of my engines for my birthday. I was constantly trying to upgrade the machine and improve it. From eleven to sixteen you were in the juniors, and I represented my country for four or five years. By the age of thirteen I had raced in several countries in Europe. Trips could be ten days to a fortnight. We couldn't afford to fly and hire a car, so we packed a tent and went on the ferry with our own car. I'll never forget one thirty-six-hour crossing to Gothenburg: the sea wasn't too kind and it seemed to take a week. My two sisters, Sandra and Gail, used to come along, but my brother Michael, who is a good few years older than I, didn't show so much interest.

I had quite a few shunts in those early days but as the speeds weren't too high it was very rarely that I got hurt and even more rarely that I broke a bone. That's why it was such fun racing, and why parents and whole families could enjoy it. They knew their kids weren't really in danger. I got pushed off the road once in Holland and hit a tree, which catapulted me about 15 feet in the air. I flew through a few branches and came down obviously quite dazed. The people around me dusted me down, said I'd be all right and told me to get back into the kart. They said they'd push me off, but when they dropped the back wheels the kart just see-sawed. All four wheels were off the ground! The framework had bowed with the impact. Their faces were a picture: I'll never forget the look of amazement. Fortunately we were able to get the kart straightened out for the next race.

I had some more painful accidents in the higher classes. I smashed some toes in my left foot and had a very bad head injury when I crashed through a wooden fence at 100 mph. It was at Morecambe. I was approaching the hairpin when the steering broke and I just took off, somersaulted and landed upside down. The helmet I was wearing had padding at the back but there was a bit of a gap in it. The impact when I hit the ground or the fence cut open the back of my head. I was admitted to the Royal Lancaster Hospital, where

I was lying asleep when a man came over to my bed. I heard him say: 'And what else can I do for you, my son, besides pray?' I realised it was a priest, but I certainly wasn't ready for the last rites. I told him where to go. Then I passed out.

That experience harmed neither his resolve nor his sense of perspective. He completed his karting days with seven Midlands Championships, a Short Circuit British title and a Northern Championship.

Through those years I never put myself up against anyone and thought 'I'm better than he is.' I've always preferred a more pragmatic approach, reasoning that given equal opportunity and equipment I could do as good a job, if not better, than the next man. At that stage I wasn't really thinking about Formula One, although I was an avid watcher and wondered how it would feel. In fact, I asked someone in F1 what it was like. He said, 'It's like shitting through the eye of a needle.' At that time I didn't know what he meant. I do now. But it was all so far out of my grasp, anyway, that there was no point in dwelling on it. If you only dream about something, you never achieve it. If you get on and do it, then at least you have a chance.

The reality of trying to achieve something you want to do is terribly frightening. In karting I went from juniors to seniors to 100cc national to 100cc international to 100cc international class 4 with gears and everything else. As soon as you start another class you start at the bottom. Just because you were a champion in the class below does not mean you have the God-given right to be as good if not better in the next class. All of a sudden you realise how much harder it is. There were a few things I hadn't won in karting but I'd certainly won my fair share, so I thought I'd have a go at single-seaters. And that's exactly what I did.

3
Single-minded

Nigel met mini-skirted Rosanne Elizabeth Perry on the road to Solihull Technical College. Rosanne, born at Northfield, Birmingham on 10 June 1954, youngest of three children, was a home economics student. She recalls: 'We lived at Shirley, within walking distance of the college.

'I was on my way one morning when a Mini van pulled up and this arrogant young man offered me a lift. He slid back the window and said "You're going to the college, aren't you?" I said I was and asked him "I know you, don't I?" I'd never accepted a lift from a stranger but I thought he was someone I recognised who lived round the corner from us. Then I looked at him again and realised I didn't know him. By then it was too late. I was already in the van and off we went. He happened to be going to the college as well. He was on an engineering course. That was how it all started.' Nigel was seventeen, Rosanne sixteen.

Rosanne says: 'I didn't know anything about motor racing. I liked horse riding and my father was a football supporter. My brother was vaguely interested in motor racing. The first race meeting Nigel took me to was at Chasewater. I didn't know what a kart was. I didn't realise it had an engine or anything like that. It was extremely cold. I wondered what on earth I was doing. But I found it quite exciting. It was a good family sport. It was a family affair. I travelled with Nigel and his family the length and breadth of the country, in the family car with the trailer and kart in tow. We were

*armed with picnics and flasks and hot soup. If it was a
particularly long trip we took the caravan.*

'From the time we started going out we saw each
other every day, I spent many an evening rubbing down
pistons or whatever. I was at Morecambe when he had
the accident and at the hospital when he had the last
rites. That gave me a new insight. I have always been
nervous watching. Word got round that I'd never been
able to watch the start. Nigel's mother was the same.
We were always turning the other way at the start. But
he was obviously good at it, he wanted to do it and
had been karting several years when I met him. I
couldn't come in and tell him he couldn't do it!'

Not that Rosanne was afraid to speak her mind. She
had opinions of her own, and their romance had to
survive a few skirmishes. Rosanne admits: 'Our
relationship wasn't all hearts and flowers from the
onset. In fact, we had a stormy relationship in the early
days. We both had strong personalities, we both knew
what we wanted out of life and tended to have a lot of
clashes. It was something of a love-hate relationship.
We had a lot of arguments but out of that developed a
lot of understanding. We were both very young and
didn't really understand it, but I think we both realised
there was something deeper there.

'There was obviously something about him that I
found attractive. I sensed what a strong personality he
had and in my heart of hearts I knew I would like a
partner with a strong personality, somebody who would
stand up to me. I think we were both a little extrovert
and he seemed able to handle me. I think over the years
our personalities have grown closer still and that is why
we now have such a good relationship.'

A love-hate relationship is exactly what it was. I think
part of the problem stemmed from the fact that I didn't
want her to get involved with some of my circle of

friends. She was a nice girl from a nice family. I'd drop her off at ten o'clock at night and then go out with my mates. It was before I went professional and like any lad of seventeen or eighteen I used to enjoy a drink and a laugh. We used to get into a few scrapes and I felt she was too good for all that. I weighed fourteen and a half stone in those days and well, let's say, was asked to leave a couple of drinking establishments. I had one or two fights over Rosanne, as well. I suppose what it came down to was that I was in love and if I found out she'd even been in the company of other lads I'd get really jealous.

Rosanne, in turn, was fully prepared to scrap for Nigel. Her spirit was amply illustrated on a holiday in Tunisia in 1970. She recalls: 'It wasn't long after his accident at Morecambe, when his head was cut open. We stayed at one of those big hotels that organise all sorts of games and competitions and Nigel put his name down for a football match, the Brits against the Germans.

'It was a boiling hot day and the pitch was really rough. The football got a bit rough as well. Nigel fell with his head near a rock and I was a little concerned. Then this big German sat on him. I was so angry I ran on to the pitch, got hold of the German by the scruff of the neck and started hitting him on the head. He turned round ready to give me a swipe but suddenly stopped and looked at me in amazement. He couldn't believe this girl in a bikini had been belting him.'

Then, as now, Rosanne was a petite lady. Nigel's frame, on the other hand, has changed drastically. His current racing weight is 11 stone 7 lb. The difference is yet another measure of his commitment and dedication. To those who have seen him only as a lean, trim, quiet family man, the image of an overweight, rumbustious youth doesn't come easily. His recollections of those times are illuminating. As he grew older, the devil

within became harnessed in his racing. When he was
young, it was given a longer rein.

When I was a kid I managed to get myself in trouble
with the Water Police within half an hour of getting a
barge on the Norfolk Broads. I couldn't stop the thing,
and almost hit them. My dad also gave me some stick
for getting too close to the bank. I was a bit mischievous
then, and as he walked along the edge of the barge I
turned straight into the bank, sending him flying over
the top. He was not too amused.

Before I was old enough to drive a car on the road,
I had a few escapades on motorbikes. For my sins I
ended up in a few ditches and hedges. I used to give a
pal of mine – a vicar's son – a lift home on the bike
from Solihull, and one day he talked me into letting
him drive. It was a big mistake. He was all over the
place, and after nearly taking my kneecaps off with a
lorry coming the other way he managed to smack a
stationary 1100 up the back. He went flying over the
car and landed on the bonnet with cuts and bruises; I
slid to the front of the bike. A woman got out of the
car, saw the blood and fainted. She thought she'd run
over him. We picked her up, told her it wasn't her fault
and walked home. The bike was a write-off.

My first car, a Mini van, used to have a rough old
time, and one night when it wasn't working I persuaded
my dad to let me use his 3.5 Rover coupe. We had a
good night at one of our haunts, but when I started up
the car to come home, the gear lever came off in my
hand. A friend of mine, who happened to be a mechanic, said he'd fix it. Fine, except that after he had,
instead of getting first gear, I was getting reverse. I
smacked my mate's car before I left the car park, which
didn't please him too much, then almost reversed into
someone at a junction. As if that wasn't enough, it

started to rain and the windscreen wiper on the driver's side flew off.

Eventually I made it home, with bent bumpers and minus windscreen wiper. I backed it up to the front of the garage and left it in what I knew was first. Then I went to bed. Next morning I was up and off to work before my parents got up. When I came back that evening my mother was waiting for me. 'What have you done to your father's car?' she said. It seems that my father had put it into neutral, then tried to select first. Instead, of course, he went backwards through the garage. It had made a mess, but luckily my dad saw the funny side of it.

My poor Mini van was written off in the end. I'd just had it repaired for about the seventh time when I got whacked up the back and that was more than it could take. The driver of the other car turned out to be an old friend of mine, too, but we fell out over that.

Another shunt, when Rosanne was driving, almost split us up. I'd gone up-market and got a 1300. With the help of a mate, I'd made it a really hot car. It was my pride and joy. I let Rosanne use it and she stuck the nose out at a junction to see what was coming. Something came all right, and wiped off the front of it. She was fine, but the car? Gone.

I had some hellish times with my mates at Lucas Aerospace. There was a huge guy called Chris Rose who was a great pal, but he challenged me to a contest to determine who should be leader. The idea was to see who could jump off a motorbike at 30 mph. I told him he could go first. I got the bike up to about forty and sure enough, he jumped off. Smash. He had to go to hospital. But we were still the best of mates.

The training officers used to check on us when we were at college full time, but more often than not we wouldn't be there. One officer tracked us down at a pub, playing darts and pool. It could have been instant dismissal, but we got off with a good dressing-down. We'd be given projects to do but used tracing paper to copy the work and spent the day playing chess. One day, though, they checked the drawers and found the chess board – with the tracing paper underneath. I was threatened with the sack.

When one professor was delivering his lecture, a mate of mine was taking the mick out of me. Finally he went too far and hit a really raw nerve. Without thinking – that was my problem in those days – I got up and hit him. We were grappling on the floor, knocking stuff all over the place.

We had some riotous fun. I used to get into all sorts of trouble. But after I met Rosanne I began to change. She cooled me down. I used to booze a lot, now I virtually never touch alcohol. I was massive then – and I mean sideways, not in height. When I went into racing seriously I became disciplined, and I trained and got rid of the extra weight.

I had a few girlfriends at the time I met Rosanne, and I expected them all to be fastened to me. I didn't like it when the shoe was on the other foot. Fortunately, whenever we fell out our friends were good enough to bring us together again. We were very young and, like all young couples, were a bit silly at times. But out of it grew a genuine, strong relationship. I think those times helped to make it for us.

Whereas I used to have some wild times with my pals, I started to go in for gentler pursuits with Rosanne. We'd still go out for a drink, but it would be *a* drink. It was the run-out into the country or to a particular spot we enjoyed. I suppose Rosanne helped me broaden my horizons and take an interest in other things. We visited ancestral homes and castles. We went to places like Blenheim Palace and toured the Cotswolds. Fuel was relatively cheap in those days and we managed to get all over the Midlands and beyond. We were still having fun, but a different kind of fun. And, unlike some of the jaunts I'd had with the lads, those outings with Rosanne were keeping me out of mischief.

I was always trying to impress Rosanne. We often went camping at Portmeirion, in North Wales, and walked along the bay. There are points where the water has cut into the rock and you can jump across to take a short cut. We came to this particular point and Rosanne suggested we jump across. She wanted to go first, but I said I'd go first and catch her. I wound myself up for this long run and as I reached the point of no return, realised I had no chance. The water was about twenty feet wide and seven feet deep. It was a lovely day, with lots of people around, and they were highly entertained. Soaking wet, I carried Rosanne back to the car.

She knew then how competitive I was, and the one thing she could beat me at was horse riding. We went pony trekking but she was so good it upset me. So I charged up the sand dunes and my poor horse collapsed with exhaustion, and rolled on top of me. I must have been overweight!

They were married at the Church of St Mary the Virgin, Lapworth, Warwickshire, on 19 April 1975. Rosanne says: 'It's a lovely old church and the vicar was super. He got us to learn the marriage vows off by heart. He felt it would mean a lot more, and it did. We both had jobs. I'd gone straight from college to work for British Gas West Midlands as a home economist and Nigel was at Lucas Aerospace. We were both working long hours and didn't see a lot of each other then.

'We had our first house in Hall Green. We hadn't really discussed family plans. Neither of us was for saying we must settle down and have a family. Our main goal at that time was Nigel's career and that was it. Children didn't even enter into the conversation. We

*were both young and enjoying our lives, our careers
and Nigel's racing.*

'We hadn't talked too much at that time about Nigel
going professional, but he had obviously thought about
it. When he asked me what I felt about buying a single-
seater car I told him that if it was something he wanted
to do I would be behind him all the way. I said I wasn't
having him going into it half-heartedly, but he was
worried about what I thought. I told him I believed he
could do it. I said that, as with anything else, we would
need a bit of luck but that we should give it a try. So
we did.'

*Nigel had joined his father at Lucas Aerospace on an
apprenticeship, and waded his way through a succession
of technical colleges to emerge with an HND in
engineering.*

I started at Solihull, then went to Hall Green, then back
to Solihull. Then I was at Matthew Bolton and finished
at Birmingham Polytechnic. Quite honestly, though, I
had no particular job in mind. All I wanted was to go
racing. My father sat me down one day and promised
me that if I got my qualifications and passed out he
would help to sponsor me in single-seater racing.

I didn't pass out until I was twenty-one. I'd got a
good job at Lucas as an electronics instructor. I went
to speak to my father in the lab there and told him I
was going racing. He asked me where I thought I was
going to get the money from. I reminded him that he
had promised to help me, but he basically said I'd got
no chance and that he wasn't going to help me. He was
adamant. I yelled at him and told him what I thought
of him. I was a married man then, living away from
home, and believed I was entitled to say what I thought.
I felt that he had deceived me.

I will never forget that day. I was bitter about it for
a long time. I'd just spent five or six years working my

butt off to qualify as an engineer, believing I would
have the chance to race cars. His heart and soul were
in karting, and he loved me going karting. He loved me
competing and winning. But frankly, I'd got bored with
it. There wasn't really much more I could achieve. I
would go along to club meetings and find it reasonably
easy to win. I'd been in the game so long I felt that as
long as my machine was working quite well, I was going
to win. It was time to move on. All I wanted was a
chance and, with or without the help of my father, I
was determined to have a go. But it was a difficult
period of my life.

Rosanne and I decided to go ahead, but my father
wouldn't speak to me and my mother was very upset
about the whole thing. They virtually disowned me for
six to nine months.

*Rosanne takes up the story: 'Someone we knew in kart-
ing had bought his own Formula Ford and was doing
reasonably well. We got talking about it and Nigel said
he wanted to have a go. He said he might not like it,
but he just wanted to find out what it was like. So we
put together £15 for an introductory course at Mallory
Park. All the others there signed up for a complete
course, but we couldn't afford that. We didn't tell
anyone else about it. Just the two of us trudged off.
That day at Mallory Park convinced Nigel he should
pursue single-seater racing and get a car of his own. I
realised it was something he really wanted to do and
from the very beginning I never put him off. I told him
I would be with him, and that is a promise I have
sustained all through.*

*'We heard about a second-hand Formula Ford that
was for sale. In fact, it was probably third or fourth
hand. Our families didn't want to know, so we went
into it on our own. We drew what savings we had, sold
whatever we could and raised about £1500. We had to*

*buy a trailer as well as the car and then we needed
something to tow the trailer. I had a nice new Mini and
we changed it for a very old Maxi so that we could tow
the trailer. The clutch kept going and I spent no end of
evenings in the garage holding the torch and rubbing
down clutch plates and things.'*

By then Rosanne, like Nigel, had grown used to the
hours of toil. They'd worked together on his karts and
when they weren't tinkering with engines and sprockets
they were out earning extra cash to finance his single-
minded obsession to go racing.

Rosanne used to give evening demonstrations for West
Midlands Gas, and after finishing at Lucas at five
o'clock I'd go to work for her brother at his business,
making picture frames. We'd work until eleven, then
go out on to the road and do the rounds of nightclubs
and restaurants, trying to sell our pictures. We'd be out
until three in the morning, and then I'd be back at Lucas
at half past seven. We did that for about three years. I
used to be so tired I'd drop off as we were driving
round.

One day, though, I got a rude awakening. I'd just got
my first ever new car, a yellow Mini clubman, and we
decided to pop over to see my grandfather. Rosanne
was driving and I was dozing when suddenly the car
came to a screeching halt. As I rubbed my eyes I looked
over the bonnet and saw a man kicking in the front of
the car. Then he jumped on the bonnet and started
hammering the windscreen and the roof. He'd gone
absolutely berserk. I shouted at Rosanne 'Reverse,
reverse', then 'My car, my car'. She was screaming and
burst into tears, but he jumped off the car.

Rosanne managed to collect herself and pulled over
to the side of the road, while I was still trying to undo
my ruddy seat belt. I managed to get it off, and said I
was going to sort out this bloke. I looked at the front

of my car. The grill was smashed, the bumper was
twisted, the bonnet was dented. My new car – I'd had
it about two days! Just as I was about to cross the road
to confront the guy, another one suddenly appeared. I
threatened to drop him, but in fact he was no problem.
He explained that the other man was his mate – from
the mental hospital.

We decided the only thing to do was to go to the
hospital. We saw the first bloke attack a parked car and
throw two bricks through a house window before we
got there. The doctors said they didn't believe our story,
but as soon as he appeared they took him away in a
strait-jacket. The police said they couldn't bring a case
against the man because he was not capable of a plea.
They said there was nothing I could do, and I had £175
worth of damage on my hands. About nine months
later my grandfather heard that the hospital had paid
for new windows at that house because one of its
employees lived there. As far as I was concerned they
had set a precedent. I went back to them and they
settled.

*Mansell's tenacity was to carry him through many a
battle in the years that lay ahead, battles that were to
be fought both on and off the track. In 1976 he was
scrapping and scraping to make the switch from karts
to cars. He would not be deterred. If karting has been
a nursery for a generation of leading drivers, Formula
Ford has been the essential junior school. This is where
you start real lessons – and often learn the hard way.
Suddenly you have 1600cc engines and a whole field of
competitors intent on becoming grown-up racing
drivers.*

That first single-seater car I had was a Hawke DL 11.
I started with a race at Mallory Park. There weren't
many top drivers there; to be honest, it was a sort of
all-comers race. But here I was in single-seater racing,

and I won. Our first race and we had a win. I was very pleased. No, I was bloody delighted. In all I had nine races that year and I won six of them. I wasn't getting carried away, but I felt I'd shown up pretty well.

Another of my wins that year was at Castle Combe. I have distinct and fond memories of that one. There were a lot of good drivers in that race and with a lap to go the track commentator was saying: 'There's a car coming up on the outside. It's got no chance of overtaking there, he's on the wrong line . . . and he's done it!' He'd obviously never seen a manoeuvre like that, but I tried it and went through to win the race.

All through my life and career I've done things instinctively. I've never idolised or tried to model myself on anyone because each and every one of us is an individual. The driving came naturally. Of course, I learned and improved with time and experience, but basically I followed my instincts. What I had to learn more than anything was how to be more of a diplomat at times. I have always been forthright and truthful and have told people what I thought. Sometimes telling people what they don't want to hear doesn't help your career. Now, fortunately, I'm in a position where it doesn't really matter anyway. Out on the track you have to be your own man and do what's best for you.

I was possibly doing things at Castle Combe that day and in other races that other drivers wouldn't have attempted or even thought about. You can't drive in any other style but your own. Even now, when I stand at a corner of a circuit and watch other Formula One cars go by I think 'Heck, that looked quick.' Then I go back to the pits and discover that I'm two seconds a lap quicker than the guy I've been watching. I'm just glad I can't see myself. Television can't really capture the speed; it's only being there, watching, that you understand it. I'll be honest, it frightens me. There are times when you think you must need a brain transplant.

Formula One cars are obviously much faster than the car I started with. You can top 215 mph in Formula One cars and corner at 180 mph or more. The top speed of my old Hawke was 120 mph. That car gave me a fairly good first year in Formula Ford. I knew then that I could win races and that, in turn, made me even more ambitious. I wanted to go on from there, to better cars, better competition. It was never a game to me: I was determined I was going to be a professional racing driver. It would mean even more hardship, more scraping for money and sponsors, but we wouldn't be put off.

We spent around £3000 on our 1977 programme and raced a number of cars. To start with we were offered a JL5 Javelin by an Irishman called Patrick Mulleady. I don't know whether he saw anything in my driving, but he must have seen my desperation. The car simply kept falling apart; quite a few wheels fell off. At Silverstone one day I was on pole position and coming round to the grid on the warm-up lap when the drive-shaft broke and fell on the track. An Irish voice said: 'Be Jesus, what's wrong with the car now?' I just threw the drive-shaft, the ball-bearings and everything else at him. I was so angry because it was yet another race we could have won.

Despite that, we did each other a lot of good. I was winning some races, and beginning to get myself noticed. He still has that old Javelin at Mallory Park and makes a bob or two giving lessons and rides in 'Nigel Mansell's former car'. Shows you what an enterprising character he is!

Formula Ford was the training ground, the way it had to be done. We used to run around from track to track in all sorts of vehicles. A friend lent us a van that was used to deliver wine. We'd sleep in the back and wake up in the morning soaking wet. The condensation was so bad that water just poured on to us. In early spring or late autumn there's no worse place than Snetterton, believe me. Boy, was it cold.

Rosanne: 'Absolutely freezing. It was like an ice box in there. We had sleeping bags and hot-water bottles, but I don't think I've ever been so cold in my life. And yet for all that, Formula Ford days were good days. There were good people, helping us and encouraging us.'

There were people like John Thornburn, who knew the sport and gave us advice and moral support. He genuinely believed in us. We had good friends called Mike and Yvonne Evans who were marvellous to us in those formative days. They used to take us out at least once a fortnight and buy us a meal. They lived about three miles from us and I used to run to their house and back. I didn't particularly like running but I had to do it, and running to their place gave me a target. I'd run there, have a chat and a drink, then run back again. One night, though, I wasn't feeling grateful for their hospitality.

Half-way home I had to cross a railway bridge, and as I approached it I saw a big, dark figure on the other side. As I got closer the figure, wearing a big raincoat, moved into my path. As I went from side to side, so did he. I wondered what the hell was going on. I thought it must be a mugger, or some clever so-and-so. All that was going through my mind when suddenly he opened his mac. He was a flasher! There he was, in all his glory. It never occurred to me to run the other way. I slowed down and then, when I was only five or ten yards from him, ran like crazy across to the other side of the road and then blasted away as fast as I could. I slowed down when I'd put a couple of hundred yards between us, and then I heard this pitter patter behind me. This bloody bloke was running after me. I couldn't believe it. I was scared stiff. I've never run so fast as I did from there to home, looking over my shoulder all the time.

It took me about ten minutes to catch my breath and tell Rosanne what had happened.

There's no doubt that the generosity and friendship of certain people helped to keep us going. Like all good parents, mine came round a bit, too. They still objected to what I was doing, but began to be a little more supportive. When I think back to the hard days I suspect that we got to the stage where, to a certain extent, we cut ourselves off from our families – partly because they didn't believe in what we were doing, but partly also because we didn't want to show them just how hard it was for us. All that effort and sacrifice, and very little to show for it. I was supposedly a professional race-car driver, but in truth I think we were a little embarrassed about our position. My wife was working eighty to a hundred hours a week, I was working all the hours God sends, we hardly saw each other, had little time for our friends, but were trying to convince ourselves and everybody else that this was the right thing to do.

In June 1977, the case against the obsession grew stronger.

I'd given up driving that Javelin. I simply couldn't go on with it. I then drove a Crossle 25F with Mike 'Abacus' Taylor. We had to build it up overnight for a race at Thruxton, but managed it and won. With his help and the help of John Crossle I then got a 32F from Ireland. It cost me nothing and I was really looking forward to my first outing with it. That was at Brands Hatch.

It was one of those situations where you have a drying track and one line. I was coming up behind a slower car, approaching a fast left-right, when he decided to brake hard. I had two options: I could hit the guy at the back or I could try to go round him. I didn't really want to hit him, so I pulled out. As soon as I hit the wet the car was out of control. I went off backwards and the whiplash was so severe that it broke my neck

in two places. I don't think I'll ever forgive him, but
then you learn from experience. I decided that the next
time anyone did that to me I'd just run into him. I never
came across that guy again, but some years later he
wrote to me saying he was the one who had put me
off. Some sense of humour!

I was taken to St Mary's Hospital in Sidcup and told
that I could be there for six months. I knew motor
racing was a dangerous game, and I'd had other accidents. But this was different. It was frightening. I was
actually paralysed for a short period of time. It was
only for a few hours, but not to have the use of your
arms and legs is a hell of an experience. The doctors
told me that I could have been paralysed permanently
or even killed. And when you see an X-ray of your own
crushed neck, it has a quite devastating effect on you.

*Rosanne: 'The worst part for me was having to leave
him down in the hospital in Kent. I could do nothing
else because I had to get back to work. I went to my
parents' house that night and stood on the doorstep in
tears. My mum could never watch a race but she was
there that night when I needed her.'*

I wanted to get out of hospital as soon as possible, so
one night I told a nurse that the specialist had said I
could sit up. Next day there was hell to pay, but I
convinced the specialist it was my fault. He said I could
have paralysed myself. The next night I did the same
with another nurse and conned him that I had per-
mission to get out of bed to go to the toilet. It took me
forty minutes. There was more trouble the next day.
They said I should be flat on my back for three months.
I disagreed – and discharged myself. Looking back, I
realise how stupid it was. But at the time, I was desperate. My wife and family were 200 miles away. I just
wanted to get back home.

I was out after about a week and was racing again

within seven. I had to wear a neck brace for racing after that, and still do. It's not totally necessary now, but when you break your neck and are warned of such dire consequences, it shakes you. It was the better part of a year before I could bring myself to head a football again. I was afraid my head might fall off! It was even longer before I could turn my head properly – I was so scared of what damage I might cause to my neck.

I was told that walking would help my recovery. Two other friends of ours, Peter and Martyn Wall, would come up from Cirencester to see me, and Peter joined me on long walks. Not that the first one was long. I had to sit down after about 25 yards. I couldn't help thinking at that time that I'd made a mistake giving up my Lucas job at Girling. I'd turned professional only a few weeks earlier. If I hadn't I'd still have been on full pay. As it was, we had only Rosanne's salary coming in.

It was during those weeks of convalescence that Nigel found another good companion – golf. Rosanne recalls: 'When Peter was with us golf often cropped up in the conversation. It involved a lot of walking and wasn't too strenuous. So for Nigel's birthday I booked him a golf lesson. I could only afford the one. He had that one lesson at Olton Golf Club, Solihull, and decided he could take to it. He got himself a set of clubs and used to be up early to queue at the municipal course. He became quite good!' He was to become extremely good. He is now virtually a one-handicap player with ambitions to play in the British Open and more. That is a subject we will come back to.

His enforced lay-off in 1977 had cost him the opportunity of more wins and more points in the Formula Ford Championship. But he returned with renewed vigour.

For all the doctors' warnings, I made a good recovery

and started winning races again. I was feeling good. I was glad to be back racing and I was driving well. We came to the last race, at Silverstone, and I still had an awful lot to do to win the Championship. I had to get pole position, win the race and achieve the fastest lap. I managed pole, got myself into the lead and then drove like crazy to make sure I had the fastest lap. Even on the podium at the end of the race, I wasn't sure who'd got the fastest lap and the Championship. Then came the announcement. I'd done it by 0.2 of a second. After all the hardship, the hassle and the injury, I had, including heats, won thirty-three of my forty-two races. And I was champion.

With Championships come prizes, and Nigel won, along with his Formula Ford crown, a weekend for two in Paris. He was to be reminded, however, that he wasn't a high flier just yet. Rosanne tells the story: 'We hadn't had a holiday for some time and had never been to Paris. We were really looking forward to it.

'First, though, we had to catch a train from the Midlands to London and then pick up a coach for Lydd Airport, near Ashford in Kent. We landed at Beauvais, miles out of Paris, so it was another coach ride. We finally arrived at our little hotel and couldn't believe it. It was dingy, grubby and we didn't even have a wash basin in the room. The beds were so bad we had to have a couple of tots of whisky before we dared get in. We didn't have enough money to book in somewhere else, so we had to stick it out. We had that long journey back, got home in the early hours with food poisoning and had to be at work again that same morning. Talk about a prize!'

I was offered a super works drive to stay in Formula Ford in 1978. It would have meant no more problems. I'd be able to concentrate on my racing and not have to worry about money any more. But I'd won the

Championship and thought, rightly or wrongly, that to stay in Formula Ford would effectively be a backward step. I had to go forward again, and that meant Formula Three. We'd had some tough hurdles already and cleared them, but they were nothing compared with what we were about to face.

4

Trouble comes in Threes

The problem with Formula Three was that it was expensive. Incredibly expensive. I'd done all right in Formula Ford, just as I'd done all right in karts. But in Formula Three I was nobody. I was starting at the bottom again. There were a lot of seasoned drivers in Formula Three. I would have to compete against people like future Formula One champions Nelson Piquet and Alain Prost. In 1977 I'd had a taste of Formula Three in a Lola which I reckon had been dug up in a garden. But that counted for nothing. If you hadn't won races in Formula Three you were a beginner, and if you were a beginner you had a hell of a job getting a drive. It came back to the same old obstacle: money.

I needed a job where I could cram in the hours in a few days of the week and have two or three days left to try to find sponsors. That, of course, would use up the money I'd just earned. It was a vicious circle. But at any rate I found some work – with our good friends Peter and Kenwyne, who have an office cleaning firm called Cirencester Business Services. Peter offered me a job which involved some administrative work and cleaning. I'd clean up sometimes at two o'clock in the morning after a party.

We had a lot of laughs. Window-cleaning could be great fun, especially in winter at 5 o'clock in the morning when the water was freezing before you could wipe it off. Needless to say, we had a lot of unofficial tea-breaks. They let me work what hours I liked – so many, as it turned out, that I could not even specify the number. In fact, you still owe me a day's holiday, Peter! They also fed me and put me up. It was fantastic moral and practical support. The trouble was that the response to my search for sponsorship was virtually nil. It was frankly a waste of time, and led to nothing but desperation. We sent out more than four hundred letters – typed out by Rosanne's sister, who was a secretary – to firms, hoping to get some backing. Replies came from 60 to 70 per cent of them, but we soon became educated in the state of the economic climate. We were told that it was 'unfavourable', and got a whole lot of other excuses I'd never heard before. There were three or four fairly encouraging replies, but even they came to nothing. In truth, we didn't even get back our money on the stamps. All we did get was the experience – probably an invaluable one at that.

We were told at the beginning of the 1978 season that if we weren't prepared to back ourselves there was no reason why a sponsor should. That fired me up to the point where I was ready to do anything to raise the money. When you are in that sort of situation you are liable to do something pretty extreme, and that is precisely what we did. We sold our apartment. Certainly it seems crazy now, but at that time we had no alternative.

Rosanne concurs: 'We were very happy at that apartment. It was our second home. It had a view of Olton Mere, near Solihull, and was really nice. Everybody thought we were mad to sell it for a few races, but we didn't care what anybody else said. We were happy taking this on together. My mum was worried, of course. We arranged to rent a house and she said she'd come round to see us when we were settled. She died before she had the chance.'

By the time we'd paid off the mortgage and everything else we had about £6000. We put it all into getting a

drive for the start of the 1978 season. The house we
moved into was dreadful. It had to be decorated from
top to bottom. We set about that ourselves and really
didn't make a very good job of it. When we were wall-
papering we got nothing to match up. We completely
botched up the lounge. It got to the point where we
were beyond caring.

*All that mattered to the Mansells was that Nigel would
be racing in Formula Three. That, surely, would justify
the madness, the botched-up lounge, everything. It
didn't. Within weeks their dreams were shattered. They
were on their knees.*

I negotiated a deal for a factory March drive. They
promised they would help me if I got funds to start off.
They reckoned they'd pick up sponsors to give me some
extra drives, but that never happened. Things began
well enough. My first race was at Silverstone and I
got pole position, ahead of Nelson Piquet and Derek
Warwick. I came second in the race and was feeling
pretty good. But the results weren't so good after that,
and quite honestly the car was junk. I had four more
races for March. I was seventh three times and I got a
fourth. They blamed me, and when my money was gone
that was it. That's all they'd been interested in.

Everything we'd built up in those five or six years
had gone in six weeks. We'd spent all we had saved
during our courting days and while we were married.
Apart from the money from the flat, we'd borrowed
some and sold everything we could. I had a pair of
guns. They were sold. So were some pictures. In all,
those five races must have cost us £8000. We were left
with nothing – no car, no house, no money. It wasn't
a case of considering packing it in. We had packed it
in! We simply couldn't race any more.

When you're left stranded like that you have to ask
yourself whether you've been a complete fool. The

money I spent with March was wasted. Totally. All it did was hurt us. That was not a good time in our lives; it was a strain on our relationship. Rosanne was working all hours and I was down in Cirencester. We were forced to split up, and that is not exactly the kind of relationship to have when you're married. In every sense, 1978 was a dreadful year. If it hadn't been for the support of Rosanne and our friends that year, I certainly wouldn't have got through.

Rosanne: 'I'm not really sure where we got our strength. In the early days we led a super life. We had a holiday every year, we had nice cars, we had weekends away and were always going out to the pictures or for meals. We gave up all that. Our lives changed completely. I didn't buy new clothes any more. I made them. It was a bad time for us.'

The only crumb of comfort was a British Drivers' Award that June, which meant I got a drive with Guy Edwards and ICI backing in a Europa Formula Two race at Donington. I was to partner Derek Daly. In practice I was beginning to get the feel of the car – and it was nice to drive – when Alex Ribeiro's March blew up, spilling oil, just over the brow as you come on to the main straight. I was the next car round, and there were no oil flags out. I went into the oil and the car just let go. I wondered what the heck was happening as I went flying off through the sand and hit the wall hard. Fortunately I was all right, although the car was very badly damaged; but I had a spare car which would have been fine for the next day.

But it wasn't quite as simple as that. Elio de Angelis, later to be my stable-mate in Formula One, came along that weekend and bought a drive with the team. So now there were three of us and, needless to say, I didn't get the spare car. It was given to Elio. There wasn't a chance of rebuilding that shunted car to handle anything like it had handled the previous day, but that was all I had. I wasn't a Formula Two driver anyway, so perhaps it didn't really matter to them whether I qualified or not. Elio was to be with them for the rest of the season. He was the one who had to qualify. It was probably better from the point of view of the team and their resources that I didn't qualify.

Guess what – I didn't qualify. Another great weekend. The first time I got into the car the steering wheel and steering column dropped in my lap, and in the end I wasn't even in the race. The people who had put up the money for my drive must have wondered whether they had value for money.

I had a couple of BMW drives in the County Championship on top of my five Formula Three races and that Formula Two fiasco, and that was the sum total of my season. This was to have been my big breakthrough year in Formula Three, but it seemed to be trying to break us. Nothing had gone right for us and we could see no prospect of a change in luck. And as if the low of 1978 wasn't bad enough, Rosanne lost her mother early in 1979. She died of a massive heart attack at the age of fifty-four. Rosanne was devastated.

Rosanne: 'I had lunch with her the day before and Nigel had popped in to see her that morning. He was often round there. He was very good to mum and she was fond of him. He came to get me from work. I knew from the expression on his face that something dreadful had happened. It capped a really horrendous year for us. My dad and I were in a terrible state and Nigel made most of the funeral arrangements. I was down for a long time.

'The thing that lifted me again and brought me back to reality was promotion at work. My senior home service advisor went off on maternity leave and they asked me to fill in. That shook me out of it. I thought

*"I've got a job to do and a department to run here"
and I got on with it. She didn't come back after having
the baby, so I applied for the job and got it. It was a
good job, one I'd long hoped for. It meant more money
for us and it gave us the momentum to get going again.'*

Suddenly, everything started to come into place a little.
Unipart were sponsoring a Formula Three team run by
David Price. He had already got Brett Riley as his No
1 driver, but the other seat was still up for grabs. I
made a couple of visits to David's business at Twicken-
ham, and I must have convinced him I was worth a try
because I got the drive. Not only that, they PAID me.
Not fortunes, of course, and I had to work for it. Part
of the Unipart deal was that I would go on a roadshow,
meeting dealers, that sort of thing. I travelled all over
England and to Jersey, Guernsey and Scotland. I had
the drive, about £25 a week in cash and a TR7 to drive
at weekends for Unipart. It meant I was again away
from home a lot, and we still very much depended on
what Rosanne brought in. But things were brighter and
I was very grateful to Unipart and David Price for giving
me the chance. I still am. That was all I ever wanted —
a chance to go racing.

We had an up-and-down sort of season. We had
Dolomite engines, and you had to drive them to believe
them. They were so inconsistent and down on power
that on some circuits we didn't have a prayer. There
was no way we were going to blow people off. We
managed only a single win, at Silverstone.

*It was the International Trophy meeting in March. On
a wet track Mansell was typically bold and led the
early stages. Then the Italian, Andrea de Cesaris, went
through and crossed the line ahead of Mansell. De
Cesaris had, however, missed the chicane and incurred
a one-minute penalty. It was Mansell's race. The win
was a desperately needed tonic for him, for Rosanne*

*and for her family. She recalls: 'My dad and sister came
along that day. Dad had never been to a race before
and he was still in a state of shock. But that bucked
him up. It bucked us all up.'*

The other satisfying part of that season came at
Monaco. I was the only driver who qualified there for
Unipart over a period of three years with six cars. I
finished eleventh. I've liked Monaco ever since. There's
something about the place, the atmosphere and the challenge of that difficult, tight circuit that I seem to respond
to.

*Through his Formula One career Mansell has consist-
ently qualified well on the streets of the Principality.
Grand Prix weekend is suitably glitzy and extravagant,
a whirl of parties and champagne receptions. It's a
millionaire's playground. These days the Mansells fly
by private jet and stay at the Beach Plaza Hotel. Formula Three days were rather different.*

*Rosanne says: 'We borrowed a dormobile and
motored down all the way to Monaco. It was quite old
and all we could get out of it was about 50 mph – and
that was with the wind behind us. I thought the journey
was never going to end. We slept in it when we were
there, and because we couldn't find anywhere to park
it we ended up putting it in the pits. We used to cook
in it, everything. The one thing we wanted, though, was
a bath. Dave Price helped us out there. He let us have
a shower in his room at the Beach Plaza. Every time
we go back there I think back to those days. I think
having gone through what we went through in the early
years makes us more appreciative now.'*

*Mansell was back at Silverstone in July 1979. The
Formula Three race was part of the programme supporting the British Grand Prix. It was an opportunity
for Formula One bosses to cast an eye over the sport's
emerging talent. The young Mansell was aware that one*

distinguished gentleman from F1 was taking particular interest in his driving.

It was there that I first met Colin Chapman, the man who had made Lotus one of the greatest names in the business. The previous season, in fact, they'd walked away with the Drivers' and Constructors' Championships. We were introduced by one of his aides, Peter Collins. I wished him well for the Grand Prix and he said he would be watching me in my race. He told me it was about time we had another English driver on the scene.

Mansell had qualified for the race in thirteenth place, immediately ahead of a young and equally ambitious French driver called Alain Prost. They were to become still closer rivals and friends in the years ahead. Collins watched at Woodcote – where the cars converged on to a tricky chicane before sweeping down the pit straight – and was impressed.

Peter tipped me off that I might be offered a test drive at the end of the season if Colin saw anything in me. They would be looking at a few drivers to find a replacement for Carlos Reutemann, who was leaving the team and joining Williams. Shortly after the race Peter said he was looking for an engineer to work for them as a travelling inspector, visiting the various factories and suppliers they dealt with. He offered me a company car (a Ford Escort 1300) plus so much a mile and so much a week. It meant making the eight-hour round trip to the Lotus HQ in Norfolk three times a week as well as all the other travelling, but it would give me the opportunity to be involved with a Formula One team and perhaps meet Colin a few more times. I jumped at it.

Mansell's 'up-and-down' season plummeted in September. The Formula Three boys were back in more

*humble company and surroundings at Oulton Park,
Cheshire. In the sport they will tell you that this is a
driver's circuit, and two drivers, Mansell and de Cesaris,
were involved in a ferocious contest behind Eddie
Jordan.*

De Cesaris had a reputation for going off the circuit,
but when I saw him in my mirrors as we approached
the turn at the end of Cascades it never occurred to me
he might try something there. The next thing I knew he
had somersaulted me. I rolled over and over until I
landed upside down, the car crushed on top of me.
When they got me out it was off to hospital again. I
had broken vertebrae, bruising and was generally badly
shaken. I wasn't too good for about six weeks after
that.

Anyway, I'd had enough of hospital and soon got
myself out of there. I wasn't fit to race for a while but
I went to Silverstone as a spectator a couple of weeks
or so later and confronted de Cesaris. Let's just say I
had words with him. We're both in Formula One now
and fortunately I have no serious problems with him.
You can't do a thing like that in Formula One. Or if
you do, you do it only once.

About a month after the accident I was at home
recovering, not able to do much and feeling thoroughly
bored, when the phone rang. It was David Phipps, of
Lotus. He said they were testing down at Paul Ricard
circuit in France the following week and wanted to give
me a run. I said that was great. He then said he'd
heard I'd had an accident and was pretty badly hurt.
'Accident!' I said, brushing it off. I told him I was fine,
no problem; I'd be there.

I put down the phone and picked it straight up again
to call the specialist. I said I didn't care what it would
take – painkillers, a corset, whatever – I was going to
have my first drive in a Formula One car the following

week. I'd got to go. Nothing was going to stop me. He gave me a load of painkillers and off I went.

I picked up a hired car at Marseilles airport and headed for Ricard. Anyone who's had to find his way out of Marseilles for the first time on his own, without a map, will know what an initiative test it is. But then I had to get into a Formula One car and try to prove myself. I stuffed myself with painkillers and didn't let on. I was afraid that if they knew they wouldn't let me drive.

The Paul Ricard circuit is perched on the white rocks of Provence, a short, twisting drive from the Mediterranean. That October morning Mansell arrived to compete with de Angelis, American Eddie Cheever, Dutchman Jan Lammers and another Briton, Stephen South, for the vacant Lotus seat. Also on offer was a test contract. A combination of hostile weather and temperamental machinery delayed Mansell's chance. Then, finally, he climbed into the cockpit of a Formula One car.

Peter Collins, an Australian who came to Britain to pursue his own dreams of a career in Formula One, had joined Lotus in December 1978 as assistant competitions manager, but the following summer was accepting the responsibilities of team manager. He says: 'I first met Nigel at Silverstone in 1978 and was impressed that he'd qualified on pole without having tested the car. We chatted for about five minutes and it struck me he knew exactly where he wanted to go. I kept tabs on him and introduced him to Colin in 1979. I'd seen him win earlier that year. He was good. He had a very positive driving style, not the most elegant, but very definite and very committed to power application, lines, etc.

'That autumn we were looking for young drivers to test at Ricard. We had a dual objective. One was to

find a replacement for Carlos, the other to find a test driver. Nigel was one of the five on our list. From what we knew of South he was a very good test driver, so he drove the development test car. The others shared the driver test car. Elio made it obvious he was the logical candidate. He had a very fluent natural style. Nigel got into the car late in the afternoon and it was jumping out of gear so his run was cut short. But he was almost as quick as Cheever and quicker than Lammers.

'*Elio got the drive and initially South was offered the test contract. South wasn't too happy and when he started to query some things Colin gave the contract to Nigel instead. I knew Nigel had taken something that day to relieve the pain, but I don't think Colin did. From that moment I had no doubts he had ability to go a long way.*

Your first drive in a Formula One car is a fantastic experience: the power, the acceleration, the feel. It was something else. I couldn't rid myself of the pain completely, but that didn't matter. I think I acquitted myself fairly well; I had only one spin.

Elio already had some F1 experience and subsequently got the drive, but Colin offered me the testing contract, along with three races. I had a foot in the door.

It was around this time that the Mansells welcomed a new member to the household and the cause. Rosanne takes up the story: '*I had always been brought up with cats, but whenever I asked Nigel about pets he said he didn't want to be tied down. Then, when he'd joined Fulford Heath Golf Club, he said there was a stray cat there that had had a litter.*

Some of them were taken home by other members, one or two of them died and eventually there was just one left. She would chase the ball on the green and play with it. She became very friendly and seemed to attach herself to me – much to the amusement of my mates. One day I picked her up, put her in a pouch in my golf bag and told her that if she stayed there for nine holes I'd take her home. When we got to the eighteenth she was still there, fast asleep. She was about six weeks old at the time and she's still with us.

Rosanne: 'Nigel picked me up from work that evening and told me to mind how I got into the car. There was a little basket with a tiny kitten in it. We called her Purdie after the character Joanna Lumley played in The New Avengers. *She's very much Nigel's cat. She sulks whenever he's ill or hurt. She wouldn't leave him when he badly injured his back in 1979.'*

It was several months later, in the spring of 1980, that I started testing for Lotus. Mind you, I thought at one stage I might have blown it. I'd been working for them during the winter and was in Peter's office a few days after the team had had a terrible meeting at Long Beach. Both cars had been involved in accidents. Colin walked in and looked me up and down. I said hello but wasn't sure he even recognised me. Then I said that I was sorry about the weekend, but still he said nothing. I asked him: 'You know what the problem was, don't you?' He just stared at me. I don't think he could believe what he was hearing. Eventually he replied: 'Okay, what was that then?' I answered: 'I wasn't driving for you.' Without saying another word, he turned and walked out of the office. I looked at Peter and said: 'I've blown it, haven't I?' Amazingly though, I hadn't. I think my cheek and the fact that I was so positive worked to my advantage. I was soon testing for him.

Collins agrees: 'That was the sort of cheeky comment Chapman himself would make. He liked people to be a little bit cheeky without being rude. I think Chapman

*saw something of himself in Nigel. There were distinct
similarities – moustache, British, both very determined,
each quite bolshy in his own way. They had a lot in
common.*

*'Before Nigel tested for Lotus in 1980, nobody else
was interested. After three days' testing it seemed he
had every man and his dog on the phone after him. He
certainly had two or three other offers to drive Formula
One cars. He was faster than a lot of regular drivers.
At Silverstone, for instance, he went quicker than Prost
in the McLaren.'*

I was given the opportunity to test at Silverstone
because Mario and Elio were unavailable. It was a
lovely day and I was to drive on the Grand Prix circuit.
Before we started, Nigel Stroud, the engineer, gave me
what amounted to a lecture and it was obvious he
wasn't a fan of mine. He told me there was no point
bolting on any aerodynamic bits until I started lapping
in 1 minute 14.5 seconds because it was supposed to
be a high-performance test. I thought: 'Well, this is
really encouraging, Nigel. Here you are in your first
Lotus test at Silverstone, the world's fastest Grand Prix
circuit, and this guy's putting you down before you
even get in the car.' I said I was sorry, but that I could
only do my best. So they bolted me in.

I said I'd take two or three steady laps and then, if
it felt reasonably good, put my foot down. On the
fourth lap I was fairly quick – or at least I thought I
was – and on the fifth I thought I was even quicker.
The trouble was that they weren't giving me any signs
on the pit wall. I thought: 'Oh no, I must be really
slow. They're fed up with me already.' I'd just done
two really hard laps at Silverstone, I was panting and I
was tired, and those were the quickest laps I could do.
I thought that if that wasn't good enough I might as
well jack it in there and then.

As I came into the pits I looked at the mechanics' faces, then at Nigel Stroud's face. They looked white, sort of shocked. I wondered what I'd done wrong. I hadn't spun, I hadn't hit anything. I looked in my mirrors to make sure I had all four wheels, and I had. I was quite worried so I parked, stopped the engine and just sat there. Nigel Stroud came over to me, bent down and said: 'I suppose you think you're bloody clever.' I was even more puzzled. Then I noticed they'd put my time on the board. It was 1 minute 12.5 seconds, the fastest time ever recorded by Lotus at Silverstone.

I think Nigel felt a bit stupid, but from that day he and I had a fantastic relationship. He's one of the best engineers I've worked with. He was very creative, what I call a doer. He didn't just talk, he would get in there and sort out any problems. I developed a very high regard for him and we worked incredibly well together.

A week later they brought Elio to Silverstone to see what he could do. He beat my time by a couple of tenths of a second. Elio then went down to Brands to test. I followed him and knocked three-tenths of a second off his best time.

I'd had two fantastic tests in a short space of time. I was as quick, if not quicker, than the regular drivers. I felt great, and said to myself 'You've cracked it.' Sure enough, Colin was impressed. It seems he was telling his people: 'This guy's not bad.' Patrick Head, with whom I would later work at Williams, was also apparently talking about me. Colin told me that after the work I'd done and the speeds I was turning in I deserved a Grand Prix. He said that with any luck it would be in Austria. A Grand Prix! I was going to get my first Grand Prix!

I also raced in Formula Three and Formula Two that year, but with mixed fortunes. While I again had little joy in Formula Three I had four Formula Two races in a Ralt–Honda and despite my previous experience with

March I was taken in by them when they said they'd give me a works drive with full backing if I found the sponsorship to get started. I put up £25,000 to £30,000 of sponsors' money and thought I drove pretty well. I should have won at Hockenheim but had fuel pressurisation problems on the last lap and had to settle for second place behind another future Grand Prix driver, Teo Fabi of Italy. From my point of view it was more valuable experience.

The most important experience, though, was my Formula One debut. Colin Chapman was satisfied that I was ready and I certainly believed I was. What had happened in Formula Three didn't matter any more. I was going to get my chance in Formula One. That was all that concerned me.

5

In the Hot Seat

The Osterreichring is one of the most imposing and spectacular of Grand Prix settings. The tarmac snakes up and down the hills, beyond the trees and back again. In 1980, with the British race at Brands Hatch, it was the fastest on the Formula One World Championship calendar. Nigel Mansell anticipated a baptism of fire on that 17 August. He didn't know how right he was.

When I turned up for my first Grand Prix I was incredibly nervous. I didn't want to upset anybody: the team, the other drivers, the organisers, anyone. I knew from the Grands Prix I'd seen that new drivers, without trying, often screwed up on the track. Suddenly you are surrounded by all these great names, people you've looked up to, and you know that when you see them in your mirrors all you're going to want to do is move out of the way and let them pass. What made it even more nerve-wracking was that it was Austria, an unbelievably fast circuit. So it was very important to do the job right.

I was in the third car, of course, because Mario and Elio were the regular drivers. They qualified comfortably enough, but my car wasn't working very well. Ten minutes from the end of the session they let me jump into Elio's car and I just made it. I qualified last on the grid. When you have the chance you have to take it with both hands, and fortunately that's what I was able to do. I was in. The following afternoon I would make my Grand Prix debut.

Sitting on the grid just a few minutes before that start I was still nervous but reasonably composed. I knew what to do. I would drive sensibly, not do anything stupid. I was fixing my mind on the job. For some reason, though, I began to feel my backside getting hot. It seemed strange and I couldn't understand why. Then I realised what had happened. When my tank was topped up, some fuel had spilt down my back and run into the seat of my car. I was getting burnt.

I told the team and they said if I wanted, I could get out of the car. I said: 'You've got to be joking. This is my first Grand Prix. I can't get out of the car. What are we going to do?' In an attempt to dilute the fuel and cool me down, they threw two gallons of water over me and my seat. It felt beautiful. Where I had been burning and stinging I was now cool and feeling great. So I started the race without any problems and for about ten laps I was fine. But then I started to burn again. The water, of course, had evaporated and I was getting chemical burns. It got worse and worse. On the corners I could blot it out because I was concentrating so hard. But on the straights the pain seared. It was like having knives stuck into me. I don't know how I drove.

I'd done forty laps when the engine blew and, I'll be honest, I don't think I've ever been as happy as I was at that moment. I didn't want to retire myself, and there's no way I was going to. But when the engine went I was so relieved. I had difficulty walking back to the pits. I had chemical burns not only on my buttocks but also on my legs, which had the effect of shortening the hamstrings. Even to this day, I have to stretch my hamstrings regularly.

I had ointment and bandages put on as soon as I got back to the pits, but by the time I reached home I was in agony. At about three o'clock in the morning I was lying in bed and couldn't stand the pain any longer. I had to go to hospital. So there I was, a little later, on the operating table at Birmingham Accident Hospital having the blisters on my backside cut off and dressed. It was a fortnight before I could sit down properly!

Conveniently, that fortnight was up with the Dutch Grand Prix. Mansell's contract guaranteed him three races that season and he was in action again at the seaside resort of Zandvoort. He qualified well, in sixteenth place, but fifteen laps into the race his brakes failed him and he went off. Another fortnight on and he was at Imola for the Italian Grand Prix. Here, however, he was unable to qualify.

Colin told me I could have another race in the last Grand Prix of the season, at Watkins Glen in the United States. Unfortunately, a week before that race there was a big shunt in Canada and Mario Andretti's car was written off. Twenty-four hours before I was due to fly out I had a telephone call telling me not to bother because they hadn't got a car for me. It was a big disappointment. We'd never been to America. Rosanne had taken time off work and we had our visas, so we decided to go over there for a holiday; we cashed in our tickets and went stand-by to Florida. We had a great time, but it wasn't what I wanted. I was supposed to be racing.

Ample consolation awaited the impatient Mansell on his return. Andretti was to join Alfa Romeo for the following season, so Chapman needed a new partner for de Angelis. Chapman was keen to take on a British driver and he was keen on Mansell. The magazines speculated for weeks, but Chapman had decided. It was to be Mansell.

Colin actually gave me the job several months before it was announced. He told me I wasn't to tell anyone and not to believe anything I might read about anyone else getting the drive. Even so, it was a difficult winter for me because I couldn't totally ignore all the articles in the motor-racing magazines. I'd read that I had no chance because of XYZ and to be truthful I began to wonder, because it made some sort of sense. It was reported, for instance, that David Thieme, whose petroleum company, Essex, sponsored the team at the time, had said that there was no way I would get the drive.

It was a crazy situation because the team owner was saying that it was 100 per cent certain I'd be driving for him, and yet the doubts were creeping in. I had to keep pinching myself and telling myself: 'Look, you're in. All this speculation is nonsense.' Sure enough, just before the season Colin announced that I was the No 2 driver and partner to Elio. It just goes to show that the so-called experts don't always know what they are talking about.

Having No 2 status didn't worry me at all. I was worried only about getting the drive. There were certainly no problems with Elio in the early part of our relationship. It was my first year – I was going to be no threat to him. Like any relationship, the second year was a bit more strained. I began to compete and show a turn of speed that he didn't like but the team did. Elio, though, was a gentleman, very mature for his years, and at the start we got on extremely well together.

What really mattered was to earn the respect of Colin Chapman. A lot of people doubted me and his decision to take me on. He was being told he was wrong, but he backed me to the hilt. He was his own man, he did his own thing. He was prepared to support a driver who was a nobody and attempt to make him somebody; that speaks volumes of the man. Lotus was the team I had always admired, but it was Colin Chapman himself who meant so much to me. He was such an inspiring man, such a strong, positive man, always years ahead of his time, a great designer a great innovator. He was

the driving force, the heartbeat of Lotus. In short, Colin
Chapman WAS Lotus.

In the two years I worked with him full time – sadly
the last two years of his life – he was not only my
employer and the head of the team, but also a father
to me. If I had a problem, I knew I could go into his
office and talk about it. Don't get me wrong. We had
our ups and downs. In fact, we had some furious rows.
But once we'd had our say that would be it. No grudges.
He was hard if he needed to be, yes, but he was fair.

*Collins confirms the mixed reception for Nigel at Lotus.
'There was resistance from a number of areas. Chapman
was happy with him, I certainly was, but a lot of people
in the team thought it was the wrong thing. I think a
lot of them reckoned it was me trying to get my mate
in.'*

*In the end Chapman had his way and Nigel was
indeed signed. The first race of the 1981 season was on
the streets of Long Beach, California. So, too, was
Nigel's first drive into trouble – and that was even
before practice.*

Rosanne and I were on our way to a sponsor's function
aboard the *Queen Mary*, which is now anchored at
Long Beach and used as a hotel. I wasn't used to driving
in America and I certainly wasn't used to the speed
limits of 35 mph on five- and six-lane freeways. Here I
was, starting my first full season in Formula One, and
the last thing I wanted was to be late for this engage-
ment. Needless to say, I decided I had to go a little
faster than the speed limit. I was weaving in and out of
the traffic, doing about 65 to 70 mph. As you can turn
right on some red lights in America, I kept doing that
to find short cuts. Then I'd stretch the law a little and,
if it was clear, go straight on at red. We were getting
that desperate.

Unbeknown to me, a police squad car had been following us for three miles, trying to catch us. We heard the siren and saw the lights when we got held up by traffic. Even then I didn't realise it was after us. I thought I'd better pull over and let him go by, but as I did so he swerved in front of us.

Two policemen jumped out, one with a shotgun and one with a .38 drawn. The one with the shotgun ran on to the pavement, the shotgun trained at us. The other came to my window with the .38 at my head. I thought 'What on earth's happening? I've seen this on television and I don't like being part of it.' I moved my hands to open the window as you would in England, but as soon as I did he shouted: 'Move your hands you sucker and I'll blow your head off.'

Rosanne and I looked at each other in horror. We were shaking. I yelled back to him: 'What do you want us to do?' He said: 'Keep your hands on the dashboard. Don't move anything.' He opened the door and made sure we had no guns, then dragged me out of the car, sprawled me across the bonnet and frisked me. He told Rosanne to stay in the car and not to move.

After he'd frisked me he turned me round, called me a few names and asked me what the hell I thought I was doing. I explained it was my first time in Long Beach and that I was there for the race. Then he screamed: 'ID, ID'. When I said I didn't understand he explained: 'Identification. Driver's licence, passport'.

When I said I was sorry but didn't have any identification he told me he could throw me in jail for that. He then told me I'd been speeding, going through red lights, etc. I asked if I could explain and when he realised we were English – and bloody frightened – he eased off a bit. The guy with the shotgun also relaxed and came round to the front of the car. I told him it wouldn't go down too well in the papers if I got thrown into jail and said the only thing I had was a St Christopher medal with my name and blood group on it.

They accepted that but said they'd still have to give me four citations. 'What's four citations?' I asked. They explained that I'd broken four laws and they would have to give me tickets. I was happy to settle for that. In fact, those two policemen, Scott and Hoss, became good friends of mine. I got them tickets for the race and they arranged for me to visit the Police Academy.

The footnote to this story I have managed to keep more or less a secret to this day. The morning after the race I was in court before the judge. What I didn't know was that over the weekend the prosecution had been retracted, but as I'd turned up with my own ticket I was fined. Without that ticket the court wouldn't have known anything about it!

We learnt a lot that weekend. We were walking round the circuit one hot and sticky day and Rosanne said she'd rest and wait at one of the corners for me. She was dressed nicely and several cars stopped and tried to lure her in. She was terrified when I got back to her. That's how naive we were. We had no idea what an American down-town area was like.

I was very nervous before the first practice session. It was my first race in America: an incredible experience. I qualified well, seventh on the grid. In the race, as can so easily happen on a street circuit, I clipped a kerb, which threw me across the road and I hit a wall quite hard. There was no major damage to the car but the rear wheel was crushed and I couldn't get back to the pits. My race was run.

The show and the drama moved from Long Beach to the beaches of Rio de Janeiro. Collins: 'It was the Sunday between the American and Brazilian races. I went to the beach with aerodynamicist and engineer Peter Wright, Elio and Nigel. I was keen on body surfing back home in Australia and quite proficient. I didn't think twice about going for a swim in the surf.

I started to try some body surfing but the waves were
so small I went out further. What I didn't know was
that there was a warning at the hotel that it could be
dangerous to swim in the surf.

'I swam out just as a whirlpool started and created
a riptide. Apparently these whirlpools came and went
every thirty minutes or so. I tried to catch a wave and
didn't go anywhere, then tried another and still didn't
go anywhere. The idea is to stiffen your body and the
wave carries you into shore. As I was getting nowhere
I thought maybe I was too far out. I tried to swim
back for twenty seconds or so but again, I was getting
nowhere.

'By this time I'd been in the water quite a while and
was beginning to get tired. I had another go, got
nowhere and realised I was in trouble. I decided to
try and attract some attention before I got into bigger
trouble. Initially, it seems Peter Wright thought I was
just messing. But when I kept waving Nigel got up and
swam out to me. By the time he got to me I was
shattered.

'He grabbed me and started to pull me in. Elio then
came out to help but the current was so strong that
after about twenty seconds he realised he was in trouble
and had to let go. As he left my heart sank, but Nigel
stayed with me and kept swimming. I was trying to
kick as much as I could but I'd been in the water so
long my arms and legs felt like lead.

'I said to Nigel "I can't go any more" but he said
"Don't give up now, kick you so-and-so." A wave
broke on to me, I got a mouthful of water and I was
convinced I was a goner. I thought "What's the old
man going to say, his two drivers killed by the surf?"
Then I thought of my wife, Jane. She was in Barbados,
two months pregnant. The baby was going to be born
without a father. Stupid as it sounds, that all went very
quickly through my head.

'As I was coughing and spluttering, saying "I can't, I can't", I suddenly felt the sand in my toes. The rip had stopped, the frequency of the waves had changed, and although I'd got water in my mouth that wave had pushed us in a little. When I felt the sand I got a new lease of life. I pushed my toes into the sand and another wave carried us in. We staggered up the beach and collapsed.

'Nigel held on to me all the way through. It was his strength and determination that saved me. No question, I would have been dead. Rosanne was on the beach looking pretty worried, but Nigel was OK, too. Then, though, Peter said Elio was still in the water. As he'd started to swim the rip had dragged him downstream. So Nigel took a few deep breaths, got up and went down to the water again. But by that time Elio had made progress and was safe.

'Afterwards my eyes and Elio's eyes were popping out, but Nigel was fine. His physical strength is very impressive. He's certainly no quitter. We learned later that ten people had drowned along that stretch of coast in twenty-four hours. We got the doctor and he said both Elio and I had strained our hearts a little, so we should take it easy. Nigel? There was no change.

'It was a long time before I went into the ocean again and even now I go in with caution. In fact, it was a long time before I went into a pool again. And I love swimming. It's hard to believe the effect something like that has on you.'

The following week Nigel had his first Grand Prix finish. He was eleventh. Elio collected two points with fifth place. Nigel's first points in Formula One were to come at Zolder, Belgium, on 17 May. It had been a tragic weekend. A mechanic was killed in a pit-lane accident; another, Dave Luckett of Arrows, was injured on the grid; and the race was held up by the drivers after two laps of confusion and protest.

In terms of progress the Belgian Grand Prix was my most important race of the year. It's just that it had to be against such a terrible backcloth. I can remember quite vividly the incident at the start. I saw everything. One of the Arrows, driven by Riccardo Patrese, stalled. A mechanic jumped over the wall to restart it. When the lights changed I was pulling away but the other Arrows driver, Siegfried Stohr, came from behind and ran straight into the mechanic and the back of the other Arrows car.

I thought he was dead and I was stunned. When the race was stopped I couldn't get out of the car. I was so shocked. Nigel Stroud, my engineer at that time, came over and I told him: 'I couldn't believe it, I couldn't believe it.' He said I should get out, have a cup of tea and settle down, but I shouted 'No, if I get out of this bloody car I'll never get back in it.'

They could see I had tears in my eyes and were so worried they called Rosanne to the car. It was all so grotesque. I started to calm down a little only when they had convinced me he wasn't dead. They told me he had broken bones, cuts and bruises, but that he would be all right. I still believe to this day, though, that if I'd got out of that car I wouldn't have been able to get back in.

When the race restarted I said to myself: 'What are we doing here? If we're here doing the job then let's make it worth it.' I had a fantastic race with Gilles Villeneuve, who was in the Ferrari. They cut short the race when it rained, with Carlos Reutemann the winner, Jacques Laffite second and me third. I had my first points and I was on the podium. It was a fabulous feeling because I'd beaten Elio hands down and for half the race I'd had Gilles breathing down my neck. For me, Gilles was an incredible driver, and I'd managed to hold him off.

The next meeting was at Monaco and that was a

huge turning point in my personal life. I was third fastest at the end of qualifying, and at a sponsor's dinner at Pinocchio's that evening Colin turned to me and said: 'You've done so well I'm doubling your retainer.' Just like that. I said: 'I beg your pardon. I don't understand.' He said: 'Listen to me, I won't tell you again. It's your last chance. I'm doubling your money.'

Rosanne and I looked at each other in amazement. Until then we'd decided that Rosanne could come only to certain races, but I told her then she should give up work and travel round the world with me. Things had changed so much in one hour, let alone two years. It became a riotous evening. Wet napkins and assorted other missiles were being thrown round the restaurant.

I didn't finish the race in Monaco (rear suspension trouble) but I got a point in Spain and things were looking good. I'd made a bit of a breakthrough and coming up soon was my first British Grand Prix. To say I was looking forward to it is a gross understatement. But unfortunately the weekend didn't go as I'd hoped.

Colin had been working on a twin-chassis car and although it had been declared illegal earlier in the season, the RACMSA, the sport's governing body in Britain, cleared a modified version. I was to drive it. Some teams protested, however, and the stewards banned it on the first day. So, overnight, we had to convert a banned Lotus 88 into an acceptable 87. The lads did a magnificent job but they simply didn't have enough time to work on it. I put my heart and soul into qualifying, but just couldn't do it.

It was was a dreadful letdown. My first British Grand Prix and I hadn't qualified. Yet again, though, Colin was marvellous. He was really upset for me. He came and put his arms round Rosanne and me. He knew we were buying a new house and that we were short on the mortgage. He asked me how much I needed to make it and I told him £40,000. He made out a cheque there and then for the whole amount and said: 'I hope this will go some way towards making up for your disappointment. I'm sorry about what's happened.'

What can you say about a man like that? He was one in a million. He had lost hundreds of thousands of pounds on the 88. I knew how much hard work and development had gone into it. He, the chief of Lotus, was entitled to be devastated, and yet he recognised that I was a victim of the situation and was able to make a gesture like that.

That gesture secured the Mansells' move from their rented house in Hall Green to their 'dream home', a pair of renovated station cottages that had become Beauchamp Cottage, Alcester, Warwickshire. Along with Purdie they now had a second cat, Gemma. Then came Abbey, a yellow labrador, followed by Kizzy, a black labrador. By sheer coincidence they were the colours of the John Player Special Lotus which Nigel drove for the following three and a half years. The family was also joined by two geese, Boris and Gertrude.

When Gertrude I died we had to find Gertrude II for poor old Boris. If you don't know how to tell the difference between a goose and a gander, I can assure you that it's not easy. My friend Peter and I had a hilarious time holding this thing upside down before we finally welcomed Gertrude II.

Mansell had to wait until the last Grand Prix of the season, at Las Vegas, to enjoy his next racing success. He came fourth, to complete the Championship with eight points and fourteenth place.

At the end of the season I felt that I could have done better. Perhaps that Zolder result had come too soon. I felt that more successes should have followed. But the important thing was that in my first year I had made

my mark as a competitive driver. People may think the
hard part is getting into Formula One, but it's much
harder to consolidate, to show you are a contender,
that you're fast and capable of going from strength to
strength.

Colin, at any rate, seemed to be satisfied with my
first year. He had enough faith in me to give me a new
three-year contract. We had finished the season with a
good result and while we were in Las Vegas Colin
and his wife, Hazel, took Rosanne and me out for the
evening. That was when I was first introduced to the
power of the buck.

The cabaret room at Caesar's Palace was busy. We
were offered places at a big table alongside other people,
but Hazel noticed some booths behind us and said they
looked nice. Colin told the guy: 'We'll have one of
those.'

The man said they were full, but Colin repeated: 'I
want a booth.' Without batting an eyelid, he started
counting out dollar bills. I asked him naively what he
was doing and he replied, 'What do you think I'm
doing?' He was, of course, tipping the man – generously! Whereupon the guy told some other people that
there had been a double booking, and cleared them out.
That was Colin. If he decided he was going to enjoy
himself, money was no object.

In the summer of 1981 our deal with Essex ended
and John Player returned to back the team in their
place. At Zandvoort we had a sponsor's function for
fifty or sixty people at a smart restaurant. What
Rosanne and I didn't know, although everybody else
did, was that I was to be the victim of a prank.

Dessert was strawberries and cream, one of my
favourites. It was all very proper, follow the top table
and all that. I was itching to start when David Way,
John Player's Special Events Manager, said to Colin

Chapman: 'Is your cream off?' Then I was warned: 'Be careful if it's off Nigel, you're racing tomorrow.'

So I put my nose to the cream to smell it and . . . splat! The sponsor had pushed my face into the strawberries and cream. I had the lot over me. All the other guests were splitting their sides. I went to the bathroom to clean up and David came in to relieve himself, so I sprayed water on the front of his trousers. Just to embarrass him a bit. All good natured, of course, but I still didn't think we were even.

My chance came at the end of the year. We had a big posh bash in Nottingham. David and Colin were at the top table, and I was at the other end of the table with the mechanics, their wives and some other people in between. For dessert we had . . . strawberries and cream.

I pulled over a waiter and asked him if he could get me a gallon of whipped cream. When I dropped him £20 he said he could. He was to leave the bowl at the far end of the room. I pointed out David Way and told the waiter that there was more money in it for him if he would ask that gentleman if he wanted extra cream.

The waiter duly asked David, who was sitting next to Colin, if he would like more cream. David said he would. I darted out of the doors at our end, up the corridor, and in through the doors at the top. I grabbed the bowl and came up behind David. Suddenly the room went silent, all eyes on me with this great bowl of cream in my hands.

David looked at their faces and wondered what was happening. Colin wondered what was happening. They both looked round to see me holding up this bowl and I thought 'Oh no, in for a penny, in for a pound,' and dropped it on top of David's head. I glanced at Colin, thinking, 'That's it, I'm fired.' Somehow, though, I was still able to say to David 'Gotcha'.

It didn't get me the sack. Instead, it started a near

riot. Colin laughed, and from that moment it was a free-for-all. I got a bucket of water to clean up David but he ducked and it went all over Colin. It was the most incredible party I've ever been to. Colin ended up with a black eye from a flying lemon.

Colin's sense of humour then seemed to go out of the window and he tried to push me out of it. Fortunately one or two people didn't think that was a good idea, and dragged him off. So then the hosepipes came out. The place was virtually destroyed. There was damage to floors, curtains and furniture. It cost a lot of money to put the place together again. My parting gift from Colin was in the pocket of my cashmere jacket – a squashed jam and custard cake.

6

The Great Divide

Peter Collins recalls that at the end of 1981 Colin Chapman was 'convinced he had a champion on his hands'. He goes on: 'Given a decent car, I think Chapman would have taken Nigel to the Championship. They had this chemical rapport. They seemed to work the same way, sometimes brutal, but they got things done.

'One day in 1981 we went roller skating. Nigel had never tried it before. Elio, however, was pretty good. He used to disco roller skate. Elio had style even on roller skates. Nigel, to start with, was flat out everywhere, a mobile accident. But after ten minutes he'd mastered staying up. It was crude, he used anybody and everybody. A lot of other people went down but he didn't. That was Nigel – just like Colin.

'Nigel had done reasonably well in 1981 and Colin was determined to keep him. When Mo Nunn, the chief of Ensign, came in for Nigel after Zolder, Colin said "No way". Towards the end of the season, in Canada, Frank Williams came looking for Colin to see if he could get Nigel to replace Alan Jones in 1982. Colin said he would rather give up Grand Prix racing than let Nigel go.'

One significant change in the Lotus camp came with the return of Peter Warr, who had spent four years working under the Wolf and Fittipaldi banners. He was brought back as team manager. Collins departed shortly afterwards, but not before he witnessed a 'clash of personalities' between Mansell and Warr.

Collins says: 'I think Peter likes to command respect

and if he isn't given it he feels offended. I think Nigel, having great belief in himself, expected more understanding from Peter. They just didn't hit it off. Nigel told Colin a few things he didn't like about Peter, and Peter found himself in trouble with Colin. From then on Peter was out to get Nigel.

'When Colin gave Nigel an improved contract I think it revved up Peter. I heard Peter comment "You'd think the guy had been in motor racing for ten years, but he's got a lot to learn." Just after Nigel left Lotus, at the end of 1984, he was widely quoted as saying "Mansell has reached the point of his very limited capabilities."

'Elio was a very charming guy and he had a rapport with Peter, while Nigel was very much the other driver. When Nigel left and Ayrton Senna went to Lotus, things changed for Elio. In 1985 he said to me "Now I understand what Nigel had to put up with." I don't think it is a conscious decision to screw the second driver, it's just something that comes across that way. There's no projection of confidence in the second driver.'

When Peter Warr came back to Lotus he could see that I had a very good relationship with Colin and I think he was basically jealous. I could speak my mind to Colin, whereas all he really did was say 'yes' and 'no'. He returned as team manager but very much under Colin.

An incident in Monaco might help to explain the situation between me and Peter Warr. He was giving Elio and me a hard time, telling us how to drive our cars, how to set them up, what tyres we should use. It got to the point where I was really jacked off. He was turning into a dictator. Things came to a head when I was waiting to do a live radio interview on the phone and he wanted me to go and talk to some sponsors.

I explained that the interview was pre-arranged and that it was for the benefit of the sponsors anyway. As

soon as it was over I'd be out there. That wasn't good
enough for him. He said: 'I'm telling you to do it now.'
That was it. I said: 'Look, unless you are going to move
me physically I'm sitting here until I've done what I
promised to do.'

Needless to say he stormed off and went straight to
Colin. As soon as the interview was done I saw the
sponsors and explained what I'd been doing, and they
understood. Later, though, I was summoned to Colin.
He sat me down, in front of Warr, and said: 'What the
bloody hell's going on then?' When I replied that
nothing was going on he told me what Peter had
reported to him, and said that he wanted to hear my
side of the story. So I said: 'Look Colin, for my money
and a bit of Elio's as well, the way he acts you'd think
he's the best engineer we've got, and the best tyre tech-
nician in the business, and why you don't put him in
the car I don't know because he must be the best driver
as well. I can't understand why you bother to employ
Elio and me. He wants to do everything.'

I told Colin that the situation was a complete joke. I
said that if Warr stuck to what he was supposed to be
doing there would be no problem, but I couldn't take
any more of this rubbish, telling me what to do all the
time and trying to tell everybody how to do their jobs.
It was screwing me up mentally.

All of this was in front of Warr, who started smashing
his fist on the table and shouting: 'That's not fair, that's
not fair.' Colin tried to calm us down and said that I
had to do as I was told. I told him that I'd signed my
contracts with him and that I'd do anything in the world
for him. But if he wanted me to do exactly what Peter
Warr told me, the only thing I could do was leave.
Being young and a bit rash I stood up and said: 'Right,
I'll go. I won't drive tomorrow. I'll give up Formula
One.'

Colin called me back and sat me down. He knew I

couldn't stand the guy and I'm sure he could see that Warr was unreasonable. He said that if I had any problems I could deal with him, but that I had to appreciate that Peter Warr was a very experienced man, so why not try to start again? I said that if Peter Warr was willing to start again that was fine by me. Peter said OK, and we shook hands.

In all honesty, though, it was never going to happen. From that moment on Peter tried to give me the kiss of death on everything. Anything he could do or say against me behind my back, he did. Quite frankly, he's one of the biggest pains I've ever come across in motor racing. The feeling was obviously mutual. He was entitled to his opinion about me and expressed it often enough. I was entitled to mine about him.

Events off the track reflected fortunes on it. The 1982 season yielded just 7 points for Mansell and he was still fourteenth in the rankings. De Angelis won a thrilling race with Keke Rosberg in Austria and wound up the year with 23 points to take ninth place. These, however, were not good times for Lotus.

The season hadn't gone as well as I'd hoped, though even years later when I had successful seasons, I was never satisfied. There are always some races where you feel you might have done better. But 1982 was a difficult year. Lotus had been dominant for so many years in the past, but they weren't at this time.

As I've said before, it's easier to get to the top than it is to stay there. Things go in cycles. Colin led the way with ground-effect cars. But when I joined the team they were in decline rather than on the up. The turbo-charged cars began getting more reliable, but we still had normally aspirated engines. Times were changing.

The season started in some confusion. The first race was in South Africa, and leading up to the meeting there was a lot of publicity about Niki Lauda's return

to racing. Then, as the weekend approached, Niki was
making the headlines for his part in leading a drivers'
strike. Didier Pironi, Niki and Gilles urged us not to
sign our super licences, which were required in Formula
One, because they felt that a certain clause would effectively tie us down to one team indefinitely. The feeling
was that we could have been exploited and had to make
a stand.

At seven o'clock on the Thursday, first practice day,
a bus was ready at the Kyalami circuit and as the drivers
turned up we were called aboard. Only Jacky Ickx and
Jochen Mass wouldn't join us. Then we were driven
off, followed by the media, and eventually we spent the
night in a banqueting room at a hotel in Johannesburg.

I didn't want to strike, especially as Rosanne was
pregnant with our first child. She was under pressure
from Colin to get me back. There was pressure on a lot
of the drivers, especially the younger ones. We didn't
want to lose our jobs, and I felt this wasn't the way to
handle the problem. Gilles persuaded me to support
the stand, and fortunately the outcome was reasonably
successful. We were later fined but that controversial
clause was dropped.

The race produced nothing for me, because of an
early electronic fault, but I got third place in Brazil after
two drivers were disqualified. My other points came at
Monaco. Between these two races came the first tragedy
of that horrendous year. Zolder seemed to be jinxed.
Gilles was killed in an accident during practice on Saturday. I was stunned. Not only was he the best on his
day, such an exciting driver, he was also a person I'd
grown to like and admire. We had adjoining pits and
often sat on the wall chatting. Like me, he wasn't one
to mince words, and we seemed to be on the same
wavelength.

The following month we were in Canada. Pironi's
Ferrari stalled on the grid and the young Italian,

Ricardo Paletti, ran into the back of him. We were told Paletti was alive, but we knew he was dead. Shortly after the restart Bruno Giacomelli, another Italian, decided he'd had enough and suddenly backed off going down the straight to the hairpin. I ran into him and as my car climbed his car I watched my hand go round and round in the steering wheel. It was broken and I was screaming.

I missed the Dutch Grand Prix and wore a brace for the British race at Brands Hatch, but it was dreadful. Again, disappointment at my home race. It took months for that injury to heal.

That August Pironi was badly injured in the wet on the Saturday morning before the German Grand Prix at Hockenheim. He never raced in Formula One again, but couldn't resist speed and competition. Sadly he was killed in a power-boat accident in 1987. Those awful events of 1982 created a terrible feeling inside me. They served to remind me that this was a very dangerous sport and I couldn't afford to play with it. I had to do it properly. You have to come to terms with the risks in your mind.

At the end of the year Colin, too, was gone. That almost finished me in Formula One. I was devastated. Totally. How could I go on without my fairy godfather? He was one of the greatest people in my life; I couldn't believe he was gone. How could he be? I was numb. The security and support I'd had disappeared. People tried to fill his shoes, but how could they? My life turned from ecstasy to hell. It could never be the same. Lotus could never be the same.

Colin Chapman died of a heart attack on 16 December 1982. He was fifty-four. Even now, though, you sense that Nigel draws strength and inspiration from his guru. Colin looks down on Nigel from a portrait on his office wall. Watching. Guiding.

As has so often been the case in his life, Nigel drew
strength that year from within his own family. On 16
August Rosanne had given birth to their first child, a
girl. They named her Chloe. A few weeks later Nigel,
Rosanne, Chloe, the cats and dogs left England to set
up home on the Isle of Man.

We had to leave behind Boris and Gertrude II, but part
of the deal when we sold the cottage was that the new
owners would take and look after them. Within a year
of being in Formula One we realised it would make
financial sense to leave England. We considered all the
obvious places. There was Monaco, which was fabulous
to visit, with a great Grand Prix, but to live there? That
was different. Then we thought about Jersey, Guernsey,
Spain and various other countries. We ended up on the
Isle of Man purely by accident.

Scott, the Long Beach policeman, was over visiting
us. I hired a plane for the day – it was a Cessna 421
Golden Eagle – and asked him where he'd like to go.
We got out the maps and he said 'What's this island?'
It was the Isle of Man. So we piled a few more friends
on to the plane and off we went. We liked what we
saw, spent the afternoon looking for properties and left
having rented a place. We put our house on the market
and within twenty-four hours we'd sold it. About five
weeks later we moved over to the island.

That first place we rented was so small that we had
to have a one-way system. We progressed from there
and have now had four different homes on the island.
It was a bit difficult to start with, leaving behind family
and friends, not knowing anybody on the island, and
Chloe being so young. But we have never regretted the
move. There's a fabulous way of life; the pace is slower,
and it's the perfect escape from the world of motor
racing.

On one of our visits to the island before we moved,

I went down with a throat infection. Rather stupidly I still went to test in Italy and became very ill. A huge lump came up on my throat. I was taken to hospital and then flown back to England. I was in hospital in England for about a week. I had acute glandular fever. My temperature went up to 107 degrees. It was very serious and I lost almost a stone in weight. It took me a long time to recover.

Through the winter months Nigel's health improved. Through the months beyond, so too did his relationship with de Angelis.

After Colin's death Elio and I became much closer, and I think that niggled the management of the team. We began to realise that I was being told certain things and he was being told other things, so we wanted to know what was going on. In the end we could see what was happening. Peter Warr had been deliberately pitching us against each other. We decided that rather than have conflict it made more sense to pool our knowledge and work together.

Eventually Elio began to have problems with Warr as well and when I was replaced at Lotus by Senna, Elio saw first hand what it had been like for me. The same sort of thing was happening to him, and he poured his heart out to me on a trip to a test at Paul Ricard.

We'd been testing at Donington and I was due to go on to Ricard. Elio, though, wasn't scheduled to drive there. Senna was to do all that test. Elio wasn't happy about it and said he wanted to go anyway and find out what was going on. He took me with him in his plane; we stayed at his father's place at Cap Ferrat that night and the next morning drove to the circuit together.

I deliberately went with Elio to the Lotus camp before going on to Williams, just to embarrass Warr and let him know I was by Elio's side and was fully aware of what was happening to Elio. The whole situation stank to high heaven. Of course, Elio still didn't get a drive down there.

De Angelis was to have an even more depressing 1983 than Mansell. The Italian mustered a mere 2 points. The Englishman managed 10 for joint twelfth place. Lotus shared seventh place in the Constructors' Championship with Tyrrell, immediately ahead of the once ridiculed Toleman team.

The first half of the season, particularly, was terrible. Elio had the Renault turbo engine but I still had the normally aspirated Ford Cosworth engine. We'd reached Detroit, in June, before I got my first Championship point. That point was a big relief to the team, too. The prize money system is such that my sixth place saved them a lot of money in transportation fees.

When we got back to Europe for the British Grand Prix at Silverstone, I finally got my turbo. The first and obvious difference was the immense change of power. When they were first introduced everybody smiled and said they'd blow up all the time. Many of them did. But their reliability record improved and people began to realise how much potential they had.

It was only when I had that Renault that I appreciated how much stronger my chances had to be with turbo power behind me. It is a matter of an advantage of hundreds of horsepower. In the early turbo days they had cooling and throttle response problems. You put your foot down and nothing happened. But things had changed since then.

I've been lucky in a sense that I have gone through many changes in my years in Formula One, all of which has been a tremendous experience. I went through ground-effect days, when the cars had strips or 'skirts' along the sides which effectively sucked them to the track. After that there was a period when the rules were being bent and skirts were being used when they shouldn't have been. Then we went from normally aspirated engines to thoroughbred turbos producing 1400 horsepower. Now, still within the span of my career, we are back to normally aspirated engines again.

From my point of view I have no preference for these regulations or this engine over those regulations and that engine. If you have the prettiest car in the pit lane and it never wins, it's a pig. If you have the ugliest car in the pit lane and it wins, it's the most beautiful car in the world. To a driver all that matters is whether he has a winner.

That summer Gérard Ducarouge, a Frenchman, joined the team as chief engineer. He built a new car in about five weeks and it was certainly an improvement. I had a new car and a new engine for Silverstone. We had problems through the weekend but in the race, my home race, I at last had a bit of luck. I finished fourth. It felt pretty good, and I needed that.

Mansell collected fifth place in Austria and, in the John Player Special Grand Prix of Europe at Brands Hatch, produced another vibrant performance in front of a British crowd. He was third on the grid (de Angelis took pole) and third in the race behind Championship contenders Nelson Piquet and Alain Prost. John Player told Warr that Mansell should stay. Despite the results, nothing had changed between boss and driver, and Mansell knew his place had been under threat. But he was attracting the attention and the headlines, and that was what the sponsors wanted.

The car was better and our performances had improved in the second half of the season. But as for the situation with Peter Warr, there was no improvement at all. Brands was great. We were quick in qualifying and I was on the podium again at the end of the race. The British public were right behind me. But Warr would have got rid of me – if he'd been able to.

He complained about me after the Italian Grand Prix at Monza because I'd backed off at the end and allowed Giacomelli to take seventh place from me. The reason I had backed off, though, was to avoid killing someone. The fans there always run on to the track when the winner crosses the line. It's bedlam. I jumped on the brakes because I was afraid I'd hit someone. We weren't even in the points! I just dropped from seventh to eighth.

One of Warr's favourite sayings was that I would never win a race while he had a hole in his backside. Well, he must be terribly constipated by now. Even his own mechanics were joking about his comment when I won my first race two years later. Warr was so two-faced he went totally over the top congratulating me. I felt like asking him about the remark, but resisted it. I just smiled and thanked him.

Speaking with the benefit of hindsight, I should have gone and started afresh somewhere else at the end of 1983. But I was still at Lotus, and would be for 1984. I was determined to be positive, and prepared myself for another season. I was going to be professional and do my job.

The Lotus had again become one of the quickest cars in Formula One, and there was cautious talk of the Championship. But in 1984 no one could contain the McLarens of Niki Lauda and Alain Prost. De Angelis would be their closest challenger, though with less than half as many points. Mansell would finish the season with 13 points and joint ninth place.

In Brazil he went off and scored nothing. In South Africa he retired with turbo trouble and scored nothing. In Belgium he had a clutch problem and had to drop out. Again, nothing. In the San Marino Grand Prix at Imola his brakes failed and he spun off. Still nothing. A quarter of the season over and Mansell was having

*to suffer a very public depression. He turned up for the
next race, the French Grand Prix at Dijon, enduring a
very private grief, too.*

Just before I was due to go out to Dijon, my mother
died of cancer. The funeral was the day after the race.
Her death left a big void in my life. She meant everything to me. She had this amazing ability to size up
people. There really was a bit of ESP about it. She could
talk to someone for a matter of seconds and be able to
work out whether he was straight or a con-man.

Whenever I had problems I knew I could go back to
her. Invariably she'd come up with the right advice. She
was also very discreet. My father couldn't keep a secret,
but I knew I could tell my mother something in confidence and that it would go no further. I lost all that.

It was a horrible weekend. We even had a terrible
flight out. Our small private plane was buzzed by a
French fighter, a Mirage. In the end a British Airways
plane came to our assistance and told us to shout
'Mayday, Mayday, Mayday'. There had been some confusion, but the Mirage was called off and we completed
the journey unscathed.

I didn't tell anyone about my mother's death. Not
even my team. I didn't want to. It was my affair, my
sorrow. Looking back, I don't know whether I should
have done the race. It's not easy to go to work the day
after someone you love dearly has died. I think, though,
that the result speaks for itself. It was a good race, a very
tough, competitive race, and I was third. The flowers I
received on the podium were on my mother's coffin the
next morning.

The next race took us to Monaco and I was very
confident throughout that weekend. It is, as I've said, a
track I relish driving on and I felt I was able to keep
the momentum going from Dijon. I made the front row
of the grid, just a tenth of a second behind Alain Prost.

Race day was wet: a rotten, wet day. But I took the
lead on the eleventh lap and was pulling away from
everybody. I was very quick. The problem was that I
was possibly too quick, and I learnt a lot from what
happened to me five laps after taking the lead. I went
off – just as a lot of other people did – and I got a hell
of a lot of criticism for that. Maybe some of it was
justified, but it's easy to be an armchair critic. Maybe
I should simply have said 'Yeah, I made a dumb mistake, I hit the barriers', and left it at that. But I told the
truth as I saw it and, as I have discovered so often in my
career, telling the truth can cause you more problems.

The truth is that I did lose the back end, and as any
driver will tell you, if you drive on a white painted line
on the road there is no grip. It's like a skidpad. I put
the power on too much, close to the white line, going
up the hill towards Casino Square, and it went away
from me. It was my mistake for sure, but I got stick for
explaining the circumstances. It happens. That's life.

Conditions were so bad that the race was stopped
after thirty-one laps. In fact, Alain was shaking his fists
at them to put out the chequered flag. He was struggling
to keep his lead.

*Mansell picked up a point with sixth place in Canada
and the roadshow moved down to Detroit. He qualified
third, behind Nelson Piquet's Brabham and Prost's
McLaren.*

Piquet didn't get away too well and there was a gap
between them. No question about it, there was a gap.
I got a good start and I went for the gap. Nelson came
across me, Alain came across a little as well and I
just got squeezed out. Suddenly there was wreckage
everywhere.

*Piquet's Brabham lurched across the track and collected
Michele Alboreto's Ferrari. Marc Surer, in the Arrows,*

couldn't avoid the remains of the Brabham. Piquet's neck was jarred, but no one was seriously injured. The Brazilian, in fact, went on to win after a restart while Mansell retired with gearbox trouble.

The problem for me then was that I hadn't won a race, while Alain was already acknowledged as a great driver and Nelson had two Championships to his name. The more experienced driver is going to get the benefit of the doubt in a situation like that, and sure enough I was made the scapegoat. I was fined six thousand dollars by FISA.

At the time I thought the fine was wrong, but it didn't do me any harm. It probably did me some good. It made me realise what I was up against, and I now appreciate that if a new driver gets up to tricks that are dangerous, the authorities have to make an example of him. You can't afford to wait for the second or third time. That may be too late.

For the benefit of the game it's best that FISA act tough, and I back them even in what they did to me. They are trying to stop further accidents. I just feel that there were another couple of drivers who should have been cautioned as well.

From the concrete-lined street circuit of Detroit, USA, the Championship scene moved to the concrete-lined street circuit of Dallas, USA. The city fathers built up their first — and so far only — Formula One festival with typical zeal. To their acute embarrassment, they then saw it almost cave in.

Dallas in July is hot. The temperature is around 100 degrees. The combination of the heat and the cars took its toll on the track. The race day warm-up practice session was early — so early, in fact, that Jacques Laffite turned up in his pyjamas — but even with the sun barely above the horizon the road surface was crumbling.

The drivers, led by Niki Lauda, demanded action . . .

or else. Heavy machinery was brought in to dig out the offending areas. Down went quick-setting concrete and on, amazingly, went the show.

Qualifying had gone superbly for us and I was very much looking forward to that race. I had my first pole position and Elio was alongside me on the grid. It was the first time in six years that Lotus had occupied the front row.

We went into the race with full tanks, while Williams ran with 50 litres less fuel. That meant, of course, that we were not only heavier but also had a higher ride height than the Williams. I led for the first half of the race, but our weight problems began to affect the handling and my tyres started to go off.

I had a heck of a scrap with Keke Rosberg, in the Williams, but just couldn't hold him. Not surprisingly, a lot of cars hit the walls and were put out of the race. I clipped a wall towards the end and lost my gears. I tried to push my car over the line, with the crowd roaring me on, but the heat and effort proved too much. I collapsed and was out for a while. When I came round I learnt that I'd been classified sixth.

He learnt also that Rosberg, a man not afraid to speak his mind, had been adding insult to injury. The Finn, world champion in 1982, condemned Mansell's 'blocking tactics' as 'unprofessional'.

I don't care who the driver is, when he steps out of the car he doesn't say what his MIND really feels. He says what his BODY feels. He hasn't had time to compute his true feelings. He can be affected by prejudice, and some time later Keke admitted that he had had preconceived ideas about me. He then said that he realised he had made an error of judgement.

Rosberg, reluctant to become Mansell's team-mate in 1985, conceded in 1986: 'I was wrong about Nigel.

*The trouble was that my opinions of him were based
on what I'd heard from other people. When I came to
work with him I found another Nigel Mansell. I'd say
that, along with Alain Prost and Jacques Laffite, he's
one of the three best team-mates I've had.'*

Keke and I are now good friends. We get on really well.
He is straight and he is also big enough to recognise if
he's been wrong. That's what makes him stand out
from so many people in Formula One. Ken Tyrrell, one
of the greatest team bosses in the business, didn't mind
admitting to me when I'd started winning races: 'I didn't
think you had it in you, but I was wrong and I'm very
pleased for you.' He's another big man.

But I could make a list as long as my arm of the
names of people in motor racing who will never admit
they were wrong about me. They still look for 'another
mistake' and don't care to mention the thirteen races I
won in a two-year period. They are embarrassed every
time they see me. I just smile to myself.

*Mansell, dubbed a 'street-fighter' in those days, had
battled largely in vain in Monaco, Detroit and now
Dallas. When the Championship returned to Europe,
he had more misfortune and gearbox trouble in the
British Grand Prix at Brands Hatch. Back to the familiar story on home ground. In Germany he was fourth,
but in Austria his engine failed him.*

*For all the hope and the promise, the season had not
gone well. Again Warr told the sponsors he wanted to
replace Mansell – and this time he had his way. At
Zandvoort, on the weekend of the Dutch Grand Prix,
he called a press conference and announced that Brazilian Ayrton Senna would be joining Lotus for the following season.*

I learnt about the deal through the sponsors. When
Peter Warr came to tell me I was able to say I'd known

about it for a long time. What's more, I wasn't at all upset. I couldn't be upset and I couldn't care less about who was joining the team, because my relationship with the man running the team was finished. I had decided I had to leave, anyway. I'd stuck it out as long as I could and there was no point in going on.

I got quite a bit of satisfaction out of the race, though. I took Elio for third place and I must say it was a nice feeling, standing on the podium at the end of a weekend like that. I didn't waste time being bitter about things, though. What was done was done. I had to look to my future. Twenty-four hours later I'd sorted it out.

Confirmation of Mansell's switch to Williams was to come later. In the meantime, he still had some unfinished business with Lotus. That amounted to only thirteen laps of the Italian Grand Prix at Monza and fiftyone laps of the Grand Prix of Europe at the new Nurburgring. The last race of the season, Mansell's last race for Lotus was the Portuguese Grand Prix at Estoril.

We were in good shape that weekend and I was looking forward to a good result to end my years with Lotus. The problem was that we had only one set of large brake pads and I, having the second car, got the smaller brakes on the front. My mechanic said there was no way my car would get to the end of the race, and he had a stand-up argument with Warr. All he got in reply was: 'Do as you're bloody well told.'

I was having a fantastic race, running in second place, when guess what? Yes, my brakes went. There were just eighteen laps left. That allowed Niki Lauda to take second place, and although Alain won the race, Niki beat him for the Championship by half a point.

Poor Alain was disappointed, but I was fuming. Warr didn't say anything to me about the brakes, but then I don't think he cared about me and I, in turn, was glad to be leaving. The whole episode of Peter Warr and what was left at Lotus was over.

7
Restart

Those last two or three years at Lotus had been rough and I'd taken more than my fair share of knocks, but it would have taken a lot more than that to dent my confidence. I could have quit there and then, left the flak behind and had a reasonably comfortable life. We'd settled in on the Isle of Man, and our second child was on the way. We didn't need any more hassle.

In fact, though, my home and family life helped me to confront the situation. I believe a stable background is necessary for success and I wanted, above all, to be successful. It was the overriding feeling I had throughout my karting days, through Formula Ford, Formula Three and Formula Two.

I'd had four full seasons in Formula One, and although I hadn't won a race I still believed in myself. I felt that given the car, the team and the backing I could win races. I needed a chance, I needed a fresh start.

Ever since my first year in Formula One, Frank Williams had shown an interest in me. He was in contact with me a number of times through the summer of 1984 and yet when Lotus took Senna I was far from certain I'd be going to Williams.

Frank had a shortlist of four or five drivers from which he would select his replacement for Jacques Laffite. He said he would make his decision at the British Grand Prix. That was in July. The British Grand Prix arrived; still no decision. Then it was going to be Germany; still nothing. Then Austria. By the time we got to the Dutch Grand Prix I'd made up my mind I wasn't too bothered about driving for Williams anyway.

After the problems I'd had at Lotus I'd decided that I would rather drive for a team who wouldn't give me aggravation and who would genuinely want me. I was talking to Jackie Oliver, of Arrows, and was very close to signing for him. He was very straight and honest, and offered me a deal. I appreciated that then, and I appreciate it now.

I decided I had to sort it out one way or the other at Zandvoort. I approached Frank and told him I wanted to know what the position was. He said he needed more time, so I said in that case I'd make it easier for him. I thanked him for considering me but told him to dial me out of the programme because it was obvious that if he'd wanted me he would have signed me by then. With that I just walked away.

Frank apparently couldn't believe I'd had the nerve to say that; but it worked. About half an hour later Peter Windsor, his public relations officer, came running down the pit lane saying: 'You've got the drive, you've got the drive.' I told Peter where to go and said I didn't want the drive, not after the way I'd been messed about. He said: 'Please speak to Frank tonight. The money is as you discussed.' I told him to get lost.

Fortunately Peter knew me pretty well and realised I was angry. He said he'd speak to me after the race. I had a good race and finished third, but I still wouldn't get in touch with Frank. I had my pride, and a few other teams were interested in me.

I began to cool down, though, and talked over the situation calmly with Rosanne. I said to myself: 'OK, your pride's been hurt, but in the morning you speak to Frank. Don't be a fool.' So I spoke to Frank and, sure enough, the drive was mine. We did the deal and that was it.

Frank and his team had always impressed me as a

thoroughly professional outfit. Williams, it seemed to me, were what a racing team should be. They were in there to win races. Their record of drivers' and constructors' championships proved they were winners. Alan Jones had won the title for them in 1980, and Keke Rosberg had taken it in 1982.

In 1984 things weren't going so well for them and that made it a good time to join them. I was convinced they would come good again. They had embarked on a project with Honda, who were supplying them with turbo-charged engines, so they were into a new era. They had started again and so had I. That, above all, was what mattered to me. It would be like a breath of fresh air.

By that time, of course, I had had plenty of turbo experience and I felt that I could contribute to the development programme. It was all part of the new challenge and I threw myself into it. The first year I was with Williams I went to Japan three times to help Honda in their engine work. Such development work takes time, but I like to think that I played my part in achieving the success that was to come. It was hard work but I knew it was essential. Williams were ambitious, Honda were ambitious and I was ambitious. Together, I felt, we would eventually get the results.

The Williams package had all the potential. It also had the backing. Canon, the Japanese camera and hi-tech electronics business machine manufacturers, were the major sponsors from 1985. The only possible problem for Mansell appeared to be Rosberg. The man who had publicly criticised Mansell's driving at Dallas soon realised that the Englishman could be his partner the following season. He registered his objection to Frank Williams – and again to the press.

Williams was unmoved, even when Rosberg threatened to quit the team rather than drive alongside Man-

sell. Williams quietly but firmly pointed out to Rosberg that he was under contract and that he, Williams, would decide who drove for the team. Mansell was signed and Rosberg stayed.

I know Keke said certain things but I also know that a lot of it was exaggerated. No matter what was said or had happened previously, though, from the moment we started working together Keke was never less than professional. On a personal level it wasn't easy and we certainly weren't friends at that stage. Yet we fought the same ground and our attitude was: 'The engine's got to be improved, so let's get on with it.'

That professionalism developed into a friendship, and our last six months working together were especially enjoyable. We could see what we had achieved together and clearly he could see me in a different light. He was able to make up his own mind about me and not have to go on what others had told him.

I learned a lot from Keke. Not only was he a great driver – a purist driver – he was also a very good, very shrewd businessman. He was very good for the sponsors. I watched how he dealt with people and projected himself. He worked at it very cleverly. That was to both his own benefit and the benefit of the sponsors. He was acknowledged as an outstanding, very fast driver. He was one of the few who could drive on the limit and still be steady. As my team-mate, he was also inevitably my yardstick. But he didn't bitch or talk about problems if his team-mate was faster. He'd just admit that on the day the other guy was quicker.

Again, that was something I took on board. You shouldn't allow it to affect you if someone is quicker on the day. What matters is to know the reason. You can have problems; you can have circuits that are suited to some drivers more than others. You have to be positive and realistic.

I was taken on at Williams as No 2 and had no illusions about my position. The spare car was primarily for Keke. If mine broke down and the spare was available, fine, I could have it. But if Keke was having problems with his car he would have first call on the spare and I would have to wait until my car was fixed.

That's the way it is in the game, and I accepted it. It shouldn't, in any case, be a significant problem if you have the right team. I have had a few differences of opinion with Williams, I don't deny that. But this I want to state: they are one of the very best teams in Formula One.

Nigel turned up for the 1985 World Championship a born-again driver. He had wintered well. He put Lotus out of his mind, enjoyed his break and looked ahead to a new chapter in his life. He had also become a father for the second time. On 4 January 1985, Rosanne gave birth to a boy. They named him Leo.

I was feeling good and reasonably optimistic at the start of the 1985 season. I had to settle in, and there was obviously work to be done. But everything, it seemed to me, pointed in the right direction. I was eager to start, eager to get on with it. I should have known, though, that it wouldn't be a fairy tale from the off.

My start with Williams was little short of disastrous. We had qualified well in Rio: Keke was on the front row and I was fifth fastest. But on the first corner Michele Alboreto, in the Ferrari, and I collided and that was effectively it. I managed to get going again but the exhaust was broken and I had to pull out after eight laps.

Next it was Portugal and there I had problems even before the start. The rain poured down on race day and as I went round on a warm-up lap I was having difficulty with the engine. It seemed I had either virtually no power at all or something like 800 to 900 horsepower –

and nothing in between. There was quite a significant lag before the power came on. Then as I went round a corner the power came with a sudden surge.

I immediately shut it off because it spun the wheels and broke the traction. It put the car into an incredible slide and in such wet conditions there was nothing I could do about it. I just sat there watching the barrier coming closer and closer until I hit it, breaking the back wheel, and bending the front suspension and front wing. I limped back to the pits and the mechanics did a magnificent job even to get the car straight again. I was able to start the race but from the pit lane, which meant I couldn't get away until the rest had. In fact, three of us started from the pit lane – an indication of how bad it was.

Several cars spun off that day, including Keke's. He had a heavy shunt coming into the main straight and cut open his hand. My race went well, though. I moved up through the field and finished fifth to pick up 2 points, only to come upon Peter Warr on the track, jumping up and down, celebrating Senna's win. I had to pull over on to the grass to avoid hitting him. I couldn't help thinking back to that business at Monza . . . A lot of people, including Keke, had been saying the car wasn't right, but I insisted from the start that the problem was the engine. It was diabolical. The Japanese took a lot of convincing but fortunately they began to listen and believe me. Once they did, they gradually got their act together and we went ahead in leaps and bounds.

The San Marino Grand Prix, at Imola, was a farce of many acts. Cars ran out of fuel with victory in sight; Prost's McLaren finished first but was found to be underweight so he was disqualified (eventually de Angelis was declared the winner). Mansell nursed home his Williams to take another 2 points.

At Monaco he was on the front row of the grid for a
second successive year but, hampered by temperamental
brakes, could manage no better than seventh place in
the race. In Canada he started from well down the grid
and picked up a point with sixth place. Next to Detroit,
and a breakthrough for the Canon Williams Honda.
Mansell started on the front row only to fall victim to
the infamous Turn Three, but Rosberg went on to win
the race.

Patrick Head, our designer, took a flier on some of the
settings on Keke's car and it worked perfectly. It meant
better traction, and with our engine you needed good
traction or else you were in trouble. It was good to see
Keke win the race. It was important for the team and
important for Honda, especially in Motor City. It
proved we were on the right lines.

*Frank Williams was moved to say: 'It's just like the
good old days again.' His team was back in the
ballpark. In France, however, Mansell was in hospital
and, by his own admission, lucky to be alive.*

We were practising the day before the race at Ricard
when I had a horrendous accident. I was doing something like 210 mph coming to the end of the mile-
plus Mistral straight towards the right-hander at Signes
when my rear left tyre exploded. It tore off the back
end of the car and, more significantly, broke the rear
wing. That sent me into a crazy spin sideways into the
barrier. As I hurtled on, the car uprooted a catch-fence
pole, concrete foundations and all. That broke the left
front suspension and threw the wheel upwards and
backwards. It glanced my head a quite severe blow as
it went by.

*Nigel was taken from the wreckage unconscious. After
a preliminary examination at the circuit medical centre
he was flown by helicopter to hospital in Marseilles.*

The following day he was allowed to leave – but for home and not the race.

That was a hell of an escape for me. I know how fortunate I was. I had blinding headaches for the next ten days or so. My ribs had taken a battering and my hand was still strapped from that shunt in Detroit. But after a big accident like that at Ricard I was very relieved to be no worse. Besides, the next race was the British Grand Prix, and I was determined to make that.

Sure enough I made it, and had a new car for the weekend. But I have to confess now that I shouldn't have driven there. The weekend was an ordeal. My body was reacting so slowly and Silverstone was the quickest circuit in the world. I really wasn't with it. Keke took pole with a scintillating lap, and I managed fifth.

Rosberg took Formula One into new territory with a lap completed at an average speed of more than 160 mph. The Finn, however, was anxious to pay tribute to his team-mate. He described Mansell's qualifying performance, just a fortnight after that crash in France, as 'absolutely magnificent'. That did not, alas, describe Mansell's feeling.

Keke told me some time later that he was complimenting me in the motorhome but that I never even acknowledged him. It was as if I didn't know he was there. But I was fifth on the grid and I was going to race. That much I knew.

I was running well in the early laps, third behind Senna and Keke, but then the clutch started playing up and after seventeen laps my race was over. I had mixed emotions. I was disappointed because things were going fairly well and this *was* the British Grand Prix. But frankly I was also a little relieved. I honestly don't know what I would have been like if I'd gone the distance.

The rest of the summer was less than spectacular for the Williams camp. In Germany Mansell was sixth, while Rosberg was classified twelfth. In Austria both went out with engine trouble. In Holland Mansell was sixth, while Rosberg again had engine failure. In Italy the engine gremlins struck again, though Mansell was classified eleventh. A depressingly barren spell, and to add to Mansell's concern he had also to contend with another tyre blow-out.

Just as at Ricard, it was the Saturday morning session and it was the rear left tyre. Luckily I was going a little slower and caught it. I had to opposite lock and in doing that I damaged my chest muscles. One way or another, I was having more than my share of problems. I had first torn a couple of chest muscles earlier in the summer during practice at Spa, in Belgium, when my steering wheel broke. We didn't race that weekend because the track, resurfaced only a few weeks earlier with a specially porous compound to cope with the usual rain, broke up in the heat! It was the first time a Formula One race had been called off.

At Monza I had to use the spare car for the final qualifying session, but I was third quickest, right behind Keke, and we looked in good shape for the race. Keke led and I set the fastest lap time. Then, again, engine trouble. It was terribly frustrating. We knew it was there; we just needed the reliability.

The show went back to Spa for another attempt at staging the Belgian Grand Prix. This time the more familiar rain clouds visited the Ardennes and the track stayed intact. So, too, did Mansell's machinery, and he took another step up the podium.

I had more problems with my chest and ribs, yet it's amazing how you can push that out of your mind when things start to come together on the circuit. In that race

things did start to come together. I knew we were
making progress; *real* progress.

Spa is one of the greatest circuits in the world – its
setting is magnificent and the drivers love the challenge
there. But it is also unpredictable. The weather can
change from one part of the circuit to another – and
that can make life very difficult.

We started on wet tyres but soon decided the track
was drying sufficiently to change to slicks. I had a
couple of moments along the way, but I came home in
second place, behind Senna. It was my best position in
Formula One. We were on the march.

*British motor racing had the bonus of an extra Formula
One race in 1985. As in 1983, Brands Hatch in Kent
would host the Grand Prix of Europe. The organisers
were rubbing their hands. Prost was poised to clinch
the drivers' Championship and a Briton emerged as a
genuine contender for victory. Mansell was composed
and cautious but yes, he sensed this might be the one.*

The result at Spa had obviously encouraged me and
then, before Brands, we had a very useful test. When
you're testing you are looking for tenths of seconds. If
you find that much you come away thinking you've
done well. In that test we suddenly found half a second.

We hadn't created any more power; it was purely an
improvement in the handling of the car. Half a second
a lap is very useful, and we were well pleased. When
you make that sort of step forward you go into a race
weekend with every right to feel you're in good shape.
Going to Brands made it better still. It's the ultimate
driver's circuit, a specialist circuit – and it's a home
circuit.

*Through the early laps Mansell ran fourth, behind
Senna, Rosberg and Piquet. Then Rosberg spun and
Piquet hit him. Piquet was out, but Rosberg made it*

back to the pits to replace a punctured tyre. Mansell,
meanwhile, had taken second place and was chasing
Senna. When Rosberg raced out of the pits, Senna and
Mansell were coming round again.

Senna had to check, and Rosberg wasn't about to
make life easy for him. Senna tried to go one way but
that merely left a gap at the other side – and Mansell
went through it. Lap nine – out of seventy-five – and
the Briton was in the lead. No Briton had won a Grand
Prix for two and a half years.

You have to be an opportunist, and what happened
ahead of me gave me my chance. I had to take it and
then keep it. There was still a long, long way to go and
anything might happen. I hadn't had a win. It was my
seventy-second Grand Prix, and it had crossed my mind
that perhaps I might be jinxed and simply not be meant
to do it. We had been trying for so long; how could I
be sure this was it?

Out there in the lead it was such a good feeling. I
managed to put myself in a commanding position and
then had to pace it. I had to consolidate, keep control,
do the job. As the race went on I think the tension
was mounting all around the circuit. The crowd was
fabulous. I couldn't see the pit-board signals through
the last few laps – I was too busy concentrating on the
driving. So I didn't really know how far I had to go.
The crowd did, though, and they gave me the count-
down signals: five, four, three, two, one . . . Their cheering and waving carried me home.

I stood on the top of the podium for the first time,
and tried to take it all in. I don't think I could, really.
But I thought to myself, 'At last. Thank goodness.
You've actually done it. You've won.' I'd gone through
the barrier, I'd arrived. That one achievement had made
it all worth while: all the effort, the setbacks and the

knocks. This was the great satisfaction, the realisation that it had all been worth it.

It had taken seventy-two races to claim that first victory, and now he knew just how good it tasted. So good, in fact, that he wanted more. He went to Kyalami, for the South African Grand Prix, hungry for further success.

I wasn't a different person, or a different driver, after Brands. It was not as clear cut as that. But I was just that bit more relaxed. I'd got a win under my belt, and people in the sport will tell you that once a driver has that he is so much better equipped to win again.

Brands was already history – a wonderful, precious day, but it had gone. I was looking ahead. I now knew the formula for winning a Grand Prix and I wanted to win more. At Kyalami I became even more convinced that I could win again. I was in pole position. You draw from every ounce of confidence, and going into the race I had plenty to draw from.

The race justified that confidence. I was under pressure from Alain but held him off, and then Keke came back strongly at the end. But I knew what I had to do and kept just enough in reserve. I crossed the line nearly eight seconds ahead of my team-mate. It was another superb day for me, and for Williams.

It all confirmed my belief that you go from strength to strength. I had had two successive wins and I'd beaten the best on offer. It is one thing believing you can do it, but quite another actually achieving it. My willpower had been rewarded, my determination justified. I couldn't see any limit to the possibilities after that. The car was good, I was on form and I couldn't wait to get to Adelaide for the Australian Grand Prix.

It was a new circuit, a street circuit, and again Mansell was on the front row of the grid, though Senna had pole. Mansell jumped ahead from the grid, only for

*Senna to fight back. Mansell's car stumbled away from
the joust and out of the race. He had a face like thunder,
but he stresses that Senna was not to blame.*

I want to put the record straight as far as that incident
is concerned. Yes, we had a bit of a scuffle but Ayrton
had no part in putting me out of the race. On the grid
the crown wheel and pinion broke. That's why I was
out on the first lap, not because of Ayrton.

It was a disappointing finish to the season, because
I'd been on a roll and was looking for another win.
Instead, Keke was the winner and I was delighted for
him. It was his final race for Williams and that was a
fitting way to go out.

He'd been great for Williams and, after our difficult
early period together, great for me. I think the team's
progress owed a lot to the way Keke and I worked
together and supported each other. We had similar driving styles and were both committed in the car. That
all made for a good understanding and a successful
partnership. I was sorry to see him go. Keke, though,
had decided on a change and was joining McLaren.

*Mansell finished the 1985 World Championship in sixth
place, with 31 points. More importantly, he had 24
points from the final quarter of the season. That was
title form. The task then was to carry that form into
1986. The prospect of the Championship challenge
loomed large in his visor. He would no longer be down
the bill in the supporting scraps. He would be a contender, a genuine contender. His team-mate for 1986?
Nelson Piquet.*

8

The Contender

Those who said Nigel wouldn't win races were probably joined by still more who were convinced he wouldn't be able to compete with Keke Rosberg. The Finn was blindingly quick, experienced, a former world champion. During the first half of the season Keke was, indeed, the faster. But in the later stages of the campaign Nigel was more than a match for him, frequently outqualifying and out-racing his illustrious partner.

Keke certainly had his engine problems, yet at the same time Nigel scarcely had a trouble-free run. What it meant in real, simple terms was that Mansell had joined the big boys of Formula One. He had confronted a champion and stood his ground. He hadn't exploded any myth about Rosberg, but had put an end to one about himself.

When Williams realised, in the summer of 1985, that they were going to lose Rosberg, their intention was to replace him with another driver of acknowledged stature. Mansell still hadn't won a race, and still wasn't regarded as a No 1. A top team demands a top name; so does a top engine supplier, and so do the top-paying sponsors.

Nelson Piquet, they decided, was just the man to fit the bill. He had won two World Championships, in 1981 and 1983, and was rated one of the best, if not THE best, in the business. He had been loyal to Brabham, who in turn had given him winning cars and unchallenged No 1 status. But now Williams were offering him the chance of a new challenge and a massive

contract − 6.4 million dollars over two years. Leaving
Brabham, his home, was a wrench, but he felt he had
to do so. In August, weeks before Mansell's first victory,
the Brazilian signed for Williams.

Nelson Piquet was undeniably a very talented driver,
already twice world champion. But I'd come to terms
with one previous world champion and I had no fears
about driving in the same team as this one. Ultimately
a driver can do the job only with the machinery he
has. It's pointless looking over your shoulder at other
drivers.

I have driven against some great drivers in my years
in Formula One − people such as Mario Andretti, Alan
Jones, Gilles Villeneuve, Niki Lauda, Didier Pironi,
Keke and Alain. At this level you have to expect to
compete against the best, so in terms of driving ability
Piquet's arrival didn't bother me in the slightest. I'd
known him since before he was world champion, so
there was nothing about him that could surprise me.

I'd heard all about his contract, and that didn't concern me either. Good luck to him; that was his business.
I knew, though, that I wasn't going to get any favours
out of him. He'd been used to getting what he wanted.
The year ahead was obviously going to have its problems, I had no doubt in my mind about that.

The first clash with Piquet wasn't long delayed.

We were out in Japan to test during the winter. Basically
I was just there playing second fiddle, literally watching
and listening to Nelson. He was prattling on, telling
everybody how he was going to win the Championship
in 1986. I said nothing; I just let him get on with it.

Nelson has a reputation for winding you up, niggling
you whenever he thinks he can show off or get a cheap
laugh. On the train, as we started the journey home, he
was sitting with Frank Williams immediately behind

me. I was still suffering some discomfort after ripping my chest and fracturing a couple of ribs. Nelson saw the chance of a little entertainment at someone else's expense. He started pushing and prodding me in the back, saying 'How are your ribs, then? How are your ribs?' He seemed to think that that was highly amusing, and presumably that he was impressing Frank. I let it go for a while and said nothing. But he wouldn't back off; he kept pushing and tapping until finally he pushed too far.

I'll take so much of that sort of thing and then I'll deal with it accordingly. It was time to deal with it. I stood up, turned round, looked him straight in the eye and said: 'You carry on doing that and I'll bust a couple of your bloody ribs for you. Then we'll see how you get on.' He backed off after that.

I wasn't going to allow myself to be wound up by anybody that winter. I wouldn't read the press and I certainly wasn't interested in what Piquet was saying. I knew people were making him favourite for the Championship and didn't rate my chances. But I didn't want to know. I was blinkered. I just looked ahead at what I had to do.

I knew what was needed to win races, and I was going to give myself the best possible chance. That meant thorough preparation and a tremendous amount of hard work. I ran miles over the hills around our home, and more back in the gym on the running machine. Swimming was another important part of the programme, along with weight-lifting and exercises.

Testing was promising and it was obvious that we were equipped to do well. There was a certain amount of confidence in the camp – a general feeling that this could be our year. The car, the FW11, looked good from the word go and it seemed to me that either Nelson or I could win the Championship. As I've said, most people reckoned it was going to be Nelson, but through-

out that testing I became more and more certain that
he had nothing I couldn't match – or even beat.

*Just before the start of the season, Williams were testing
at Paul Ricard circuit in France. It was the opportunity
for a little fine-tuning, a chance to complete the minor
details of preparation before the team flew to Rio for
the Brazilian Grand Prix. All was set. The team was
content, the drivers were content. Frank Williams, with
Peter Windsor alongside him, drove away from the
circuit contemplating a season of success.*

Everything seemed perfect, everything was ready. We'd
be in Rio the following week and were confident that
we would be competitive. That final test had set us up
nicely. Frank had left before us and must have been
well pleased. Then this guy came running down the pit
lane towards our garage. 'Come quick, come quick,' he
shouted, 'Frank Williams has had an accident.'
    We stopped our test instantly. Nelson, our aerodyna-
micist Frank Dernie and I all jumped into a car and
raced to the scene of the accident, about fifteen minutes'
drive from the circuit. We found Frank and Peter
Windsor in a field, both out of the car. Peter seemed
all right, but Frank was bleeding profusely. He was
obviously badly hurt.
    Frank was taken to hospital in Marseilles and we
stayed up all night, just waiting for news. It was a
horrific accident and for some days Frank was fighting
for his life. It's strange, though, the effect that something like that can have. It brought us all closer together.
We shared our anxiety, and at the start of the season
we were pulling as one.

*Frank Williams came through those critical days. He
had always been a fitness fanatic and that probably
saved him. The day after he was due back from Ricard,
he was to have trained with double Olympic 1500m*

champion Sebastian Coe. The athlete was one of very many who called, anxious to find out about Frank's condition. The outcome was that Frank would live, but would be confined to a wheelchair.

The following year Frank, back at the helm, said: 'The trouble was that I could never resist going for a corner. Patrick Head had told me often enough what would happen one day. It was a million per cent inevitable I would go off. I know I should have had a chauffeur for the previous three years but I didn't, and sure enough I had my crash. Driver error. Full stop.'

The way the team carried on and went through that season is a credit to Frank Williams. There are many departments at Williams and they all took on the responsibility of running themselves. Patrick Head took overall charge and did an exceptional job. He was outstanding in the role, just as he has always been an outstanding maker of cars. I have a lot of admiration for the man, not only for what he did that season but for what he has given Williams over many years.

In Rio, qualifying underlined the fact that our prospects were good. I was third on the grid, Nelson second. Senna was on pole. That meant I had two Brazilians right in front of me, the two drivers who would be desperate to do well in front of their home crowd.

Nelson didn't get away too well, so I was straight through into second place and right up Senna's rear wing. We were still on the first lap, approaching a left-hander at the end of the back straight, and I'd pulled out and got myself alongside him. He was pumped up and started wheel-banging.

My mistake was in trying to pull back. I should have held my ground, because if anyone was going to go off it was Senna. He was on the outside. Instead, he got away with it and I was off. I was again out of the race on the first lap. With 20–20 hindsight it's easy to look

back and handle the situation. But Senna is not a driver
to take lightly. There are times when he can be very
dangerous. It was another lesson. Life is one long learning curve, and you never reach the end.

Nelson went on to win the race, and that showed
that our optimism had been justified. When we went to
the new circuit at Jerez for the next race, the Spanish
Grand Prix, I was even more determined. I was also
looking to get in some mileage. I'd done virtually
nothing in my previous two outings.

It was a good weekend and a cracking race. I chased
Senna through the closing stages, chopping back his
lead, and dived for the line off the last bend. But he
just got the verdict. I was disappointed not to make it,
yet perhaps it proved to the team and everybody else
that I had the same turn of speed as the so-called hero
who had just joined us.

*Senna beat Mansell by 0.014 seconds, officially the
second smallest margin of victory in Formula One history. The gap between Peter Gethin and Ronnie Peterson, in the 1971 Italian Grand Prix, was recorded at
0.01 seconds. With less sophisticated equipment available then, times were taken only to hundredths of a
second. So it cannot be certain that the Gethin–Peterson
finish was, in fact, closer than that between Senna and
Mansell. Lotus calculated Senna's winning distance at
93 centimetres.*

*At the San Marino Grand Prix Mansell lined up, for
the third time in three races, behind the two Brazilians.
He was never, however, to be in the contest, which was
won by Prost.*

I had an ignition problem right from the start and I was
soon back in the pits. After eight laps I had to call it a
day. It was an up-and-down start to the season. That
drive at Jerez – which I think surprised a few people –

demonstrated the possibilities, but then I was back to an early retirement.

It was good to get to Monaco for the next race; my liking for the place seems to increase every year. Qualifying again went pretty well for me and I made the front row of the grid. Alain just pipped me for pole, Senna was third and my team-mate eleventh.

I was making a habit of qualifying on the front row at Monaco. The problem was that I'd never been able to get a good result there; I was pleased just to finish. Alain won, followed by Keke and Ayrton, and I was fourth. It was a result – that was something.

On the Wednesday after Monaco the teams were at Paul Ricard circuit testing. Elio de Angelis, who had left Lotus and joined Brabham, was out on the circuit. Suddenly he lost control. His car cartwheeled, eventually landed upside down and burst into flames.

I was in the pits at the time and saw the smoke and the fire. We thought an engine had blown. But then there was a lot of frantic activity, people running and shouting for fire extinguishers. The look on their faces made it obvious that this wasn't just an engine fire. It was serious – and perhaps someone was still in the car.

I ran towards the smoke and the fire but it was still a good few minutes before I got there, and I couldn't believe Elio was still in the car. Worse still, no one was doing anything. Alain and I tried to get close to the car but as we moved closer it started to crackle and bang. The heat and the smoke forced us back. It was horrific. When they finally got Elio out, Keke and I drove his girlfriend to the hospital.

It is estimated that Elio was trapped in his car for eight minutes. Then there was a lengthy delay before a helicopter arrived to take him to hospital in Marseilles.

Elio died the following day, 15 May 1986. He was twenty-eight.

Elio's death hit me very hard. He was a gentleman, and despite our problems in the early days, he had become a friend. A lesson should have been learnt, but it wasn't. The drivers tried to get improvements in safety standards, but the only really positive action at Ricard was the alteration to the circuit. They took out the loop where Elio had had his accident.

The drivers, journalists and other observers that fateful day claimed that the safety precautions were inadequate. Some marshals were said to have been in shorts and T-shirts instead of protective clothing. It was not an 'official' test and no emergency helicopter was at the ready. At the French Grand Prix, less than two months later, drivers again complained about the standard of the marshals.

I won the next race, in Belgium, but it wasn't a win I could really enjoy. Elio's death cast a cloud over the entire weekend. Out on the track, though, you have to do the job. As on one or two previous occasions in my career, my perspective was sharpened. Again I told myself that if I was going to do it, I was going to do it well. Otherwise, there just wasn't any point.

Before the race I felt we were looking good, but over the last few laps we were concerned with fuel. Patrick Head was shouting on the radio: 'Watch the fuel.' It was close, but we had just enough. From the point of view of the team and my Championship prospects it was a satisfying win, but it wasn't one to celebrate. I was, at least, able to dedicate it to Elio.

The Canadian Grand Prix, however, gave me real cause for satisfaction. Montreal is one of those circuits that so many drivers like. You'd hear a lot of them, especially my team-mate, say: 'This is my favourite track. I'm quick here.' I kept hearing that all weekend, and the more I heard it the more content I was with my own driving.

Canada and Detroit came together – two races on consecutive weekends. Very different circuits, but one trip, and in my mind I set myself a target of 12 points from the two races. I thought that was realistic and that it would put me nicely on course for the Championship. I didn't want to think too much about the title itself. I just wanted to be driving well and to be on course.

Montreal was one of those weekends when everything seems to gel. I was on pole, went away at the start and led comfortably. My only concern was fuel consumption. I backed off for a few laps and didn't mind Keke taking the lead. Then, when I was happy about the fuel situation again, I stepped up the pace, overtook Keke and went on to win.

The rest of the 'Big Five' stayed the course but all were trailing in his wake. Prost was second, Piquet third, Rosberg fourth and Senna fifth. Senna had actually been lapped. Mansell's performance was one of immense authority. Watching his driving, observing his easy manner throughout the weekend, you sensed he had truly come of age.

My confidence was fairly high when we went on to the street circuit in Detroit. I was on a hat-trick of wins and was joint second with Senna in the Championship. two points behind Prost. Senna took pole but I was alongside him on the front row. That was fine.

Senna led for a couple of laps and then I blasted through. Everything was looking good again. Then I started having braking problems, and Detroit, with its narrow track and concrete walls, is no place to have braking problems. I held the lead for five laps but couldn't hold it any longer.

From then on it was a case of just hanging on, nursing

the brakes and hoping to pick up some points. Senna won, Alain was third and I was fifth. We'd dropped valuable points, but in the circumstances I had to be positive and view it as 2 points gained. My team-mate threw it into the wall when he was charging, but that's so easily done, particularly on a circuit like Detroit.

I had another couple of points, and sometimes you have to accept that winning is out of the question. As I know only too well, the Championship is all about collecting enough points and not necessarily winning most races. I'd picked up 11 points in North America and I returned to Europe feeling we were going all right.

Next came the French Grand Prix – at the Paul Ricard circuit. I have very mixed memories of that place now, but before that weekend they were mainly bad memories. My accident, Frank's accident, Elio's accident – all were connected with Ricard. It seemed that there was some horrible sort of jinx over the place.

But once you are there, you must remember that you are a professional. When you are doing your job you have to clear your mind of all those bad memories, and that weekend I was there to do a job. If you are not professional in a Formula One car there is only one person who gets hurt, and that's you.

Senna and I again shared the front row of the grid. The changes to the track brought the first corner much closer and there was some concern among the drivers that there could be problems there. But I got through it without any trouble and went clear, into the lead. Then a bit of good team planning came into play.

We had reckoned that the race would be hard on tyres, so we decided to make two stops for fresh rubber. That would enable us to maintain our pace and, we hoped, be in a position to win the race. The pit crew operated magnificently and everything was spot on. On both occasions, I came out and took back the lead from Prost. I crossed the line seventeen seconds ahead.

*Piquet was third and Rosberg fourth. Senna had spun
off on oil. The top of the Championship read: Prost 39
points, Mansell 38, Senna 36, Piquet 23. Prost had no
doubts about the identity of the man he had to fear. 'It
is Nigel,' he said.*

*Mansell's third victory in four races had lifted him
within reach of the World Championship summit. Victory in the next Grand Prix would take him there. And
that next Grand Prix? It was the British, at Brands
Hatch, just one week away.*

The build-up that week was something I'd not experienced before. For the first time I was going into my
home race a proven winner. If you are a British driver
in a British team, the whole country seems to know
about it, and the moment we arrived at Brands I sensed
that expectations were high. There was tremendous
interest from the fans and the media.

I knew Patrick was a little concerned that it might
get too much and affect my performance, but I was
relaxed and very composed. I wasn't even bothered
by talk of my possibly joining Ferrari. I was certainly
thinking about it, but it wasn't weighing heavily on my
mind at that stage. I was also approached by McLaren.
In fact, I was being spoken to by three or four teams.
Far from troubling me, that, frankly, made me feel
good. It was a measure of my success. It's nice to be
wanted. In any case, the crowd and the entire weekend
were phenomenal. The only thing on my mind was the
British Grand Prix.

*Frank Williams made an emotional appearance that
weekend and his drivers paid him the perfect tribute.
In qualifying Piquet was fastest, Mansell second. In the
race a crowd of 115,000 would witness the pair stage
a classic duel – but only after a dramatic incident forced
a restart.*

I got off to a fabulous start and then, as I changed from first to second . . . bang! The drive-shaft had broken, and I thought to myself: 'That's it. I'm out of the race.' It was a shattering feeling. I'd got away so well, everything was right, yet now all I could do was pull over and let the rest of them go by. I screamed at my team on the radio. I was totally dejected. Then, to my amazement, out came the black flags. The race was stopped.

What I didn't know was that behind me, at Paddock Hill Bend, the first corner, there had been a big accident. Thierry Boutsen had lost it, bounced back off a barrier, and as other cars tried to avoid him there was a pile-up. Poor Jacques Laffite went off and crashed head-on into the barrier. He was trapped for half an hour and taken to hospital with broken legs. It was a terrible day for Jacques, but a lucky one for me. I had another chance.

It meant a new race, and although there wasn't enough time to repair my car, we had the spare. Nelson had first call on the spare but didn't need it, so it was mine for the race. We didn't have a drink bottle fixed in the spare, but I was just glad to be in the race. What happened after that was a fairy tale.

It was Nelson's spare car and he had set it up for himself. I hadn't been in it all weekend. It's not quite the same when it's not yours, so I was uncertain how it would handle. Nelson was away first, and Gerhard Berger jumped ahead of me for a couple of laps. Once I started feeling comfortable and confident in the car I moved up to second, and from that moment it was really down to a head-to-head with my team-mate.

I moved up to him and tracked him. I knew by then that the cars were well matched. It was a question of not making mistakes. On that particular day he made one mistake; I made none. It was to make the difference between winning and coming second. He missed a gear on lap twenty-three, and in a situation like that a missed gear can make or break you. I took my chance and sailed by.

Then it was my turn to try to hold him at bay. When I came out of the pits after my tyre change, I was just ahead of him and knew that as long as he wasn't alongside me there would be no problem staying in front, not with three corners coming up. As long as I didn't make a mistake there was no way he was going to overtake me. I just had to hold my line and once my tyres had warmed up I'd be on my way again.

There was still a hell of a lot of racing to do, of course. He was right behind me for lap after lap but I never allowed him to break my concentration. No one else was anywhere near us. We were the only two who completed the full seventy-five laps. All I had to do was maintain that form and the race would be mine.

The tension brought an eerie hush over Brands on that warm July Sunday. Every time the two drivers swept away from that great amphitheatre that forms a considerable section of the circuit, the spellbound audience wondered whether they would be in the same order when they returned. Always they were, but always Piquet was menacingly close, trading blows and lap records with the Englishman – until, with the laps running out, the Brazilian began to fall back. The feeling of relief coursed through the stands. Piquet was broken. Mansell was going to win.

I could sense the euphoria in the car. I was carried home by waves of cheering fans. The previous year at Brands had been very special, and yet this one surpassed it. It was such a hard race. I'd never had to drive at that speed so consistently. The pace was relentless. I hadn't had a fluid bottle and was worn out at the end. I didn't feel too steady at the top of the podium, but I knew where I was all right – I was on top of the world.

That evening we had a party with friends and rela-

tives at our hotel, Brands Hatch Place, and I began
to enjoy the feeling of being the leader of the World
Championship. We watched the highlights of the race
on the news. Yes, there was the confirmation: I *was* on
top of the world.

The very next morning, though, it was back to reality.
We were testing at a small track in northern France,
Croix-en-Ternois, and I had to be up early. That's
motor racing – the last race is history; what matters is
the next one. Testing is the part of motor racing that
the public doesn't see. This is the really hard work,
away from the television screens and the crowds.

*Also out of public view, Piquet was complaining to
Frank Williams. He had already claimed that Mansell
was getting preferential treatment. Now he argued that
as No 1 driver, he should have been allowed through
to win the race. Williams was unmoved. There were no
team orders, and that was the way he wanted it. His
was a RACING team. How, in any case, could the team
have restrained Mansell in front of his home crowd? It
would have been impossible.*

*Relations between the two drivers had not been good
from the time of that first confrontation on the train in
Japan. From this triumphant British day at Brands, they
were to grow steadily worse.*

It never surprised me to learn that Piquet had been
complaining – he bitched and complained a lot about
everything. That's the way he is and it's his problem,
not mine. I never allowed him to bother me; I just
looked after my own business.

*The following weekend Nigel's business took him to
Maranello, the home of Ferrari. Inevitably, the story
broke out in the Italian press. He had been to meet
Enzo Ferrari himself. Would he be driving their beloved
red car the following season?*

I spoke to Mr Ferrari and had lunch with him. I was very impressed with what he and his team had achieved in the past and what they were aiming to achieve in the future. I signed minutes of the meeting setting out the terms of a proposed contract for 1987 and 1988, but I later decided that the time wasn't right. I wouldn't, however, rule out the possibility of my driving for them in the future.

By the time we arrived in Germany for the next race, both Williams and Honda were pressurising me to sign contracts. They wanted to make an announcement to the press. At that stage I didn't want to sign; I wasn't ready to sign. From my point of view there was no reason to rush it. I wanted time to think, but everybody else wanted everything done yesterday.

To say, though, that the Ferrari business affected my racing that weekend is rubbish. What did affect me was the car breaking underneath and losing downforce. People may say that I was lucky to finish third because the two McLarens ran out of fuel. But it could also be said that I was unlucky, because if my car had been all right I would have won the race. It was simply a bad race weekend.

Victory went to Piquet, second place to Senna. But in the Championship, Mansell's lead had increased to 7 points. The next race was a first for Formula One: the action took place behind the Iron Curtain, in Budapest, Hungary.

We had a new circuit and I decided I would sign a new, two-year contract with Williams. I figured, after virtually being told by various people close to the team that if I left I would throw away my Championship hopes, that I really had no choice. Based on that logic, I signed.

There were other reasons, though. I had had success with Williams and I do believe in a bit of loyalty. I turned down more money by not going to Ferrari and, with the benefit of hindsight, it could be argued that I should have gone. Maybe I should, but money isn't everything. That weekend, anyway, it was a relief to have signed with Williams. I just wanted to get on with the racing and the Championship.

At the end of the first qualifying session I was fastest, but after the second I was fourth, a couple of places behind Piquet. That night he was bragging to some people that he was going to screw me in the race because he had found a technical advantage I didn't know about. They didn't know whether it was his usual wind-up or that he had actually got something. The proof of the pudding was there for all the following day.

I was never going to beat him: his car was far superior. I came third, behind Piquet and Senna. I was furious because an adjustment he'd made to the differential had given him far better grip. I didn't have the facility to try it, and the information wasn't passed on to me. We were supposed to be in the same team, after all!

I had one of my first big rows with Patrick Head over it. He said that the adjustment had made no difference at all, and that I'd driven badly.

Frank Dernie said that Nelson was a better driver and that it was his kind of circuit. They said I was causing my own problems by the way I was driving. That was rubbish, and I think I put the record straight there the following year when I took pole and led all the way until a wheel nut fell off.

I'd like to think that it was just a misunderstanding, and that the misunderstanding was caused by Nelson, not by the team management. It's certainly fair to say that there was embarrassment in the team because they got a lot of bad publicity over it.

I had made my point in no uncertain terms, and I went to Austria the following week determined to put the episode behind me. I was still 7 points clear in the Championship and felt I could extend that lead. I was fastest in the warm-up and second behind Alain when I had a drive-shaft failure. But for that failure I would have had 6 points, and possibly 9, to take home. Alain's car only just made it to the line, but he had a win. The result that day was to prove vital to the Championship.

The top of the table before the Italian Grand Prix read: Mansell 55 points, Prost 53, Senna 48, Piquet 47. Mansell was third on the grid behind Teo Fabi, in the Benetton, and Prost. Just before the start the front-row pair discovered problems. Prost changed cars and started from the pit lane, and Fabi lined up at the back of the grid: Mansell was effectively on pole.

Prost was actually disqualified for changing cars too late, while Senna had been left stranded on the grid with transmission trouble. The only Championship contenders in the action were the Williams pair.

I had half a seat belt come off, which made driving very uncomfortable, so I was quite content to pick up second place and 6 points that day. I applauded my team-mate because he did a better job, and as long as he's beaten me fair and square I'll admit it. He'd won the race, but I was leading the Championship by 5 points.

When we got to Portugal things were back to normal: he was into his wind-up routine again. At the circuit he was taunting me with things like: 'Be careful you don't crash on your way to the hotel' and 'Senna will have you off at the first corner.' I simply replied: 'Look pal, it's you he'll be holding up because I'm going into the lead from the word go and I'm staying there.' That shut him up, and he certainly wasn't saying much after that because it went exactly as I had told him it would.

I had a spare car at Estoril, which enabled me to try out one or two different things and prepare more thoroughly. I was fastest on Friday and although Senna took pole on Saturday I was quite satisfied being on the front row. I was first into the first corner, opened up a gap and held it.

It was a masterful drive that relegated the rest to a frantic squabble for the places. Prost was second, Piquet third and Senna a struggling fourth. It was the young Brazilian's last show of defiance. With two races remaining, the Championship was down to three drivers, and the expressions on the faces of Prost and Piquet suggested they had scant hope of stopping Mansell.

From a driver's point of view I suppose that race was as near perfect as you are going to get, and it set me up with a 10-point advantage. That gave me a good chance, but I couldn't afford to think I had the title. There were two other good drivers still there and 18 points to go for. One mistake, one little fault on the car and it could all change. Anything could happen.

As Mansell headed for Mexico City's first Grand Prix in sixteen years, Frank Williams confessed his astonishment at the English driver's emergence among the elite. He said: 'When we took Nigel on it was as a good journeyman and a good team man who would get points and win the odd race. I'm in wonderland now.' He reflected the feelings of many.

Mansell had fine-tuned his preparations for the high altitude challenge of Mexico City with a productive test in Austria. He was not, however, prepared for the mishaps awaiting him.

For starters he was thrown off the back of a pick-up truck by his co-author! Nigel drove a couple of laps of the circuit, then handed over the steering wheel while he climbed on the back for a better view. Approaching a corner his co-author saw in his mirrors a hire car steaming up. Driving the car? Mr Piquet. The only

*decent thing was to move over – wouldn't want to be
accused of blocking him! But you know what it's like
once you're off line: no grip, sideways ... Oops,
where's Nigel? On the track rubbing his leg and shouting things like, 'What the bloody hell's going on?'*

*Then he was visited by the infamous Mexican bug.
The Williams mechanics, ever considerate, placed an
arrow on the ground next to Nigel's car. The arrow
pointed to 'toilet'. Worse still was to come in the race.
He was third on the grid, behind Senna and Piquet;
Prost was sixth.*

What happened at the start was nothing short of a
nightmare. It was a horror story, but it was true. And
it was happening to me. The cars settled on the grid,
the red light went on, and I stuck it in gear. The light
turned to green and, to my astonishment – nothing. All
I'd got was a bunch of neutrals and I was going
nowhere. I couldn't understand it. First I was angry,
and then I was gripped by fear: somebody could hit me
up the back.

Fortunately I wasn't hit and managed to creep from
the line in second gear. By then at least twenty cars
were ahead of me. From that moment it was a case of
getting what I could. I was able to pull myself up
through the field, and finished fifth. That was some
consolation, and I still had a good lead in the Championship with only one race left.

*The result could have been worse. Gerhard Berger, in
the Benetton, won his first race, followed by Prost,
Senna and Piquet. As a driver counts only his best
eleven scores in the Championship, Mansell and Prost
now had to drop points. Mansell's 2 points from
Mexico were wiped away. He went to Adelaide still
on 70, with Prost on 64 and Piquet on 63. The title
permutations for the Australian Grand Prix were end-
less, but one simple fact was clear: third place for Man-*

sell would make him champion no matter what the others achieved.

In a situation like that you look at the percentages and think things look good. The whole build-up to the race was perfect. Rosanne made the trip with me and shared some of the psychological pressure. As soon as I arrived in Adelaide I played golf with Greg Norman, who is one of the best in the game, of course, and now a good friend. I got lucky a couple of times and actually outdrove him. That set me up and I was nicely relaxed right through the week.

Qualifying couldn't have gone better. I was fastest in both sessions. Piquet was second fastest, Prost fourth. I'd made up my mind I wasn't going to break any records. If the win was there for the taking, fine. But there was no need to take any risks, no need to get involved in anything. A nice secure third place was all I needed and all I wanted.

Menacing clouds closed in on Adelaide that Sunday, 26 October 1986. An umbrella protected Mansell from the light shower as he sat on the grid, motionless. The rain eased and the cars snaked round the street circuit on the formation lap. Back home much of the nation was up in the middle of the night, eyes on the box. Britain was ready to acclaim its first world champion since James Hunt, a decade earlier.

This time I got off to a good start, but for the first time in my career I could afford to take it easy. I would stay out of trouble and let things settle. I was fourth at the end of the first lap. Piquet was leading, Senna second, Rosberg third and Prost fifth. As the race took shape, though, I was running third, Rosberg was in front, Piquet second. Prost had had a puncture and was now fourth. It was all going according to plan.

Suddenly though, on lap 63 of the 82-lap race, Keke's

Blazing a trail in the Williams, Canada, 1985

Piquet has to bow to his team-mate's winning style, British Grand Prix, 1986

Top: Greatest triumph – heading for the line in the 1987 British Grand Prix. *Above:* Centurion! Nigel makes his 100th Grand Prix appearance in Austria, 1987, and marks the occasion with victory

With Greg Norman
at Silverstone, 1987

Taking on the
golfing giants at the
1988 Australian
Open

Proud dad with Ferrari Testarossa and son Leo

Greg and Chloe showing dad the way

Happy family – Rosanne, Leo, Chloe, Greg and Nigel with Abbey and Kizzie

Harbour master, Monaco 1987

Splashing to a splendid second place at Silverstone, 1988...
... and the acclaim of his fans

Nigel makes his debut for Ferrari in Brazil, 1989... and the pit crew play their part...

… in a dream victory

tyre went and the whole picture began to change. All he could do was park his car at the side of the track and walk away into retirement. I had wanted to stop for tyres at half distance but, because Nelson chose not to, the team decided I should stay out and radioed me to tell me not to come in. Goodyear had told us the original set would go the distance and there was no distinct drop-off in performance, no reason to suspect there was anything wrong with the tyres.

I didn't know, however, what had happened to Keke. All I was aware of was the fact that his car was at the side of the circuit. If I'd known he'd had a blow-out and I'd had the chance to come in for fresh rubber, I would have done so immediately. Although Alain went through to take second place I was still third with more than a minute in hand over the fourth driver, Stefan Johansson, in the Ferrari. The team realised they had to call me in and planned to do so after the next lap. But it was too late. We never got the chance to change those tyres.

As I came down the long straight for the sixty-fourth time, my rear left exploded. I was in sixth gear approaching 200 mph. The car was jerking out of control. At that moment all that concerned me was self-preservation. All the way down the straight I had to wrestle with the car to keep it out of the wall.

Then, as all this was happening – the rubber shredding away, the sparks flying – it hit me: I had lost the Championship. It had been in sight and now it was gone. The car bumped into the wall in the run-off area at the end of the straight and I was safe. I was alive. But when I climbed out of the cockpit I looked at what was left of my tyre and just hung my head in my hands.

I have had my share of disappointments and I no doubt have more to come. But that was, without doubt, the biggest disappointment of my life. It was very hard to accept, because I'd done everything right. It was all

going beautifully, I was totally in control – only for it
to be snatched away from me.

*Nigel Mansell's Championship, like that tyre, had disin-
tegrated 44 miles short of the line. Anxious Williams
officials brought in Piquet for new tyres. Prost, forced
to change earlier because of that puncture, went clear.
Piquet charged, but it was a forlorn charge. Prost took
the flag and, for the second successive year, the Championship. He was on 72 points, Mansell 70, Piquet 69.
The Frenchman generously conceded: 'Nigel was the
one who deserved it most.'*

When we walked away from the circuit, Rosanne, too,
was very low. All through my career we had worked
together for this day, this opportunity. To have the
Championship stolen like that was a terrible blow to
both of us. It wasn't just a personal disappointment,
though. I was disappointed for all the people who had
helped us and all those who had stayed up to watch
back home in Britain.

Even now it's depressing to recall what happened on
that day. I had five wins that season, more than any
other driver, and had been so close. Sick as I felt, I had
to pick myself up and tell myself I could do better still
the following season and that the experience would
stand me in good stead. Winning the BBC's Sports Personality of the Year award helped. I knew the British
public appreciated what I'd done. I would be back.

9

Running Battle

Before Nigel Mansell returned to the Formula One World Championship, he went back to his father's home in Wythall. The visit ended in conflict with his step-mother and banner headlines in the press.

In the summer of 1986 my father decided to phone me to say he was going to re-marry. That was a shock in itself, as Rosanne and I didn't even know the woman he was talking about. Then, in the next breath, he said he was going to marry her the very next morning. I was upset, as I think many people would have been in my situation. My mother had died little more than two years earlier, and my father's new fiancée was about twenty-six years younger than he was. Not one member of the Mansell family went to the wedding.

But at New Year 1987, Rosanne and I decided we'd try to keep the family together and call on them to wish them well. We couldn't say we liked what had happened, but accepted that they had their own lives to lead. Rosanne had never met my step-mother, and I'd seen her only once when I bumped into them at an airport in Paris on my way back from Mexico.

When we arrived they were obviously surprised to see us, and my step-mother said: 'You'll have to forgive me, I'm rather inebriated. I've had too many sherries.' I really wanted to speak to my father anyway, but she kept butting in. My father asked her half a dozen times to leave the room and let us talk, but she wouldn't. The problem is that she's wearing the trousers.

I told my father that although we'd made the effort to call, there was no point staying; we'd go. My step-mother then said she had something to say, and she started slagging us, saying I should be doing this, that and the other, and offering advice on how I should be treating my father. What really hurt was when she said that it was *her* house, that my mother wasn't with us any more. We had obviously made a big mistake in going there.

I walked past her as we went along the corridor to the door, and suddenly she was on the floor yelling how she was going to tell the world about me and ring the papers. Everything was contrived. We thought it was just the drink talking. But the next thing we knew there was a big story in the papers and we had the press at our gate.

It hurts all the more because, no matter what, my father is still my father, even if something of him died when my mother died. I don't believe he is the man he was, because he is under the spell of his new wife. But whether or not we get on any more is our own personal business.

The business of supplying tyres to Grand Prix teams became the sole responsibility of Goodyear in 1987. Gone with the competition were the controversial qualifying tyres. Turbos were two years from extinction; there would be boost restrictions and pop-off valves fitted.

The power produced by the turbos and the cost of backing up the technology involved were becoming so phenomenal that something had to be done. Unless you had a multi-million-pound budget it was becoming impossible to compete. No one likes racing knowing there's no chance of winning. The result should be better racing, and cheaper racing.

The qualifying tyre effect will never be completely

scrapped, because even a new set of race tyres gives you only two or three really flying laps. But ridding the sport of the out-and-out qualifying tyre was a very sensible move. As for fuel restrictions, it is part of the test to get the maximum out of what you have.

I was less impressed with the introduction of sliding-scale fees for super licences. It meant that successful drivers were to be penalised for their success. I didn't mind a flat rate, as with any other licence, but to be charged up to around £7000 was, many of us felt, unfair.

As Mansell set out for Rio and the first race of the season, Alain Prost was leading a drivers' stand against the fees. The drivers, fearing increased charges in 1988, said they would not pay, and the race was under threat. Inevitably, a compromise agreement was reached. The fees would be index-linked. Mansell, meanwhile, had other problems.

I was due to fly on the Wednesday evening with Varig, the Brazilian airline. They discovered a fault in the navigation system that afternoon and we were still waiting late that night. Then we were told there would be no flight until the following day. So we motored to Coventry from Heathrow, took a private plane to Madrid and connected with a Rio flight there. I arrived about twelve hours before practice.

It can't have affected me too much, though, because I stuck the car on pole. The race didn't go anything like as well. I had a huge overheating problem which gave me no chance of sustaining the pace. Then I had a puncture, which was a joke because I was so slow I didn't see how I could have got a puncture! I don't think I've ever worked so hard for one point.

Nine points for victory went to world champion Prost, six for runner-up to Mansell's team-mate Piquet.

That was a setback, but I wasn't too dismayed because we clearly had winning potential, which is all you can hope for. Any thoughts about the Championship can come later. Before you actually start racing you really can't know whether you have a winning car. At the second race, the San Marino Grand Prix at Imola, we began to get a clearer picture.

It was a mixed weekend for the team. During Friday's qualifying session Nelson had a substantial crash, hitting a wall sideways at 180 mph. He was taken to hospital badly shaken and with a slight foot injury. On medical grounds he was ruled out of the race, but he was very lucky he wasn't badly hurt. All credit to designer Patrick Head; several drivers – including me – have had massive accidents in his cars but come away relatively unscathed.

With Nelson out of the session it was decided, quite rightly, that it would be unethical for me to go out and try to beat his time, so we concentrated on full tank work in preparation for the race. On the Saturday we tried one or two things and that allowed Senna to take pole, but I was still on the front row.

On the second lap of the race I had the lead and it soon became obvious the main pressure would come from Alain. Fortunately for me it was one of those rare days when his car had problems and he had to pull out. From that moment on I basically had to do a good management co-ordination job with the pits to ensure we didn't run out of fuel. Imola is one of the worst races of the year for fuel consumption. I kept a healthy lead over Senna and made sure I won at the slowest possible pace. That should always be the strategy.

The victory put me on top of the Championship, but after two races I was hardly going to get carried away. It was better than being at the bottom, but as well we knew it's the position at the end of the season that matters. The important thing was to be winning again and going in the right direction.

Piquet, employed that race day by an Italian television company to comment on proceedings, watched stern-faced as his partner clinically extracted his 9 points. Spa, scene of the Belgian Grand Prix, offered the prospect of another Mansell win. He was on pole, with Piquet alongside. Senna was third on the grid, Prost sixth.

I made a fantastic start and began to build up a useful lead, only for the race to be stopped because of an accident involving the two Tyrrells. When we got off again Senna barged his way through, but that wasn't a serious problem. I decided I'd wait for the straight to take him.

Then, for some reason, he slowed coming out of the long left corner. He may have missed a gear, or the engine may not have picked up as he changed. It's not beyond all reason that Ayrton might have tried a dirty trick and just dabbed the brakes and come off the throttle. These things happen in racing, and everybody knows there's no love lost between us. But whatever he did, it gave me the opportunity to pass.

There's no question that with anybody else we wouldn't have touched and I would have been through without any problems. But I think he was incensed and tried to make or break at the next corner. He came up on the inside and punched us both off.

I took a lot of criticism for that incident, but if you look at Senna's line he'd got it totally wrong. He didn't even attempt to brake in the right place. He was far, far too tight. We can all be irresponsible at times, and on that occasion I certainly felt that he was. Let me make this clear: the manoeuvre was forced upon me. He slowed to such a degree that I had to brake and pull sideways. You don't have time to debate or you're hitting him up the back and having a big accident. I

chose to pull sideways and was suddenly alongside and
going by.

He was out of the race there and then and although
I got back on, the car's underside was damaged. It was
terrible on fast corners. I made a pit stop to have things
checked and went out again. But the car was just not
right and I scared myself crazy. At every corner I was
hanging on for grim death. I radioed the team and asked
them to look at the bodywork as I went past the pits.
They told me to maintain a comfortable pace, but
eventually Patrick called me in. He had no alternative;
I would have retired anyway.

When I came in I was raging with fury. I felt I'd done
nothing wrong and yet was out of a race I knew I could
have won. Worse still, I'd frightened the hell out of
myself just trying to keep going. I'd had two previous
conversations with the guy over similar incidents, and
still he was giving me problems.

For the first time in my life I experienced a red mist
coming down in front of me. I went to the Lotus garage
to tell Senna what I thought of him. I didn't hit him,
but I got hold of him by the collar and pushed him up
against a wall. I cannot deny that three or four Lotus
mechanics dragged me off him.

It made a big story in the papers and, of course, I
was the bad lad. What wasn't reported was that as I
was held off he stood in front of me and threw punches
and kicked me several times. I was so angry I didn't
feel a thing, but the next day I had a sore spot on my
chin where I'd obviously been caught.

I am not, for one minute, condoning what I did and
I am not trying to justify my actions. I am merely
explaining precisely what happened and why. But someone had to do something to that guy and subsequently,
coincidence or not, I haven't had one bit of trouble with
him since. If anything, he's become almost the perfect
gentleman. I think I made my point so forcibly that

he'll think twice about doing anything silly with me again. But he has certainly matured.

A lot of the problem stemmed from the fact that we had both always been competitive, we were both usually at the front of the grid and were both fairly hard chargers. Therefore, we always found ourselves too close. Other people weren't having the same problems with him because they weren't competitive enough or quick enough to be up there with him.

For all the stick I got over Spa, FISA saw no reason to take any action against me. There were suggestions that I should be fined for bringing the game into disrepute, but the sport's governing body did not agree.

Piquet also had to drop out of the race, leaving Prost a simple route to equal Jackie Stewart's record of twenty-seven victories – and to the top of the Championship. When the show arrived in Monaco for the next presentation the attention and pressure were inevitably on Mansell. If anyone thought that would put him out of his stride they were mistaken.

My entire weekend was perfect until the thirtieth lap of the race. It's difficult to talk in terms of perfection, but my best lap at Monaco was one as near perfect as I've managed. I never feel more alive on a race track than I do at Monaco. Everything has to be synchronised, everything working together at incredible speed.

Coming out of the tunnel it's very easy to run close to the barrier. It's the same coming out of Casino Square. On a very quick lap you just clip the barrier. I wouldn't say it's so much scary as exhilarating. My best lap was truly exhilarating.

It stunned onlookers and rivals alike. His time of 1 minute 23.039 seconds was seven-tenths of a second faster than second-placed Senna and 1.7 seconds faster than Piquet, who was third. Piquet conceded that he

*could not compete with his team-mate on that form.
He argued that Mansell took too many risks, and
pointed out that Monaco was not one of his favourite
circuits anyway.*

For all of us there are circuits where we find that our
car doesn't work so well. Sometimes you just can't
pinpoint the reason. In my case that makes me try all
the harder to make it work. If you tell yourself this
track or that track is not a favourite, then you have a
weakness.

It seemed that we had no weakness at all that weekend. I got away nicely from pole, built a lead and just
sat there. I cruised with so much room to spare between
car and barrier it was easy. I didn't even break sweat.
Just as in qualifying, the race was as near to perfection
as I'd achieved. But then the exhaust broke up and so
did my race. Quite obviously that exhaust system
should not have got through quality control. A comfortable 9 points gone. Frustration wasn't the word.

*Those 9 points went, instead, to Senna. Piquet picked
up 6. Detroit was to take a similar course, and to raise
questions about Mansell's physical condition.*

For some time before Monaco and afterwards I had the
sniffles, and it became obvious it wasn't just a cold.
Detroit was coming up and I decided to get a medical
opinion. Tests showed I was allergic to a whole list of
things, including pollen, grass, early blossoming trees,
feathers and rabbits. I was put on anti-histamine, which
was perfect – except that it dried out my system.

So I toddled off to America, played golf in the heat,
went through practice and, although I was a bit groggy,
wasn't really bad. I was on pole, again ahead of Senna
and Piquet, and went clear in the race. By the midway
stage, though, I felt dreadful. I started getting cramps
and it was all I could do to keep going and finish fifth.

In two hours of racing I lost the best part of a stone in weight, and it was all down to those tablets. The subsequent talk about drugs was utter rubbish. When I came home I stopped the tablets and was fine.

Senna completed the Detroit street race on one set of tyres to beat Piquet and Prost across the line. Mansell was down to fifth in the Championship. He desperately needed a good result in France, and responded with typical commitment. He dominated every practice and qualifying session, claiming his fourth successive pole position.

My only anxiety in the race was caused by a piece of debris I picked up lapping a backmarker. It wrapped itself around the front wing of my car, which gave me understeer and imbalance. I tried to wiggle it off and even told the pits I might have a deliberate spin to get rid of it. They weren't too impressed with that idea! When I came in to change tyres the crew ripped it off and I had a well-balanced car again.

Ayrton was never really in contention that day, and I'd managed to hold off Alain when he was pushing. It came down to me and Nelson. I knew he planned another stop so I kept him out as long as I could, never pulling too far away. Finally he went in and charged after me with fresh rubber, but I had enough in reserve. I'd won in the slowest possible time. The race had gone according to plan.

That demonstration of mature race-craft gave him a second successive victory at the Paul Ricard circuit. Now, as in 1986, he headed for his home Grand Prix with Britain agog. The top of the Championship table looked like this: Senna 27 points, Prost 26, Piquet 24, Mansell 21.

After winning at Brands Hatch in 1985 and 1986 it was a bit much to expect to do it again in 1987. This time it was at Silverstone and, even with a new corner at Woodcote, it's an incredibly fast circuit. There was an enormous build-up to the weekend and as if that wasn't enough, Piquet did his bit to stir it, stressing that he'd *won* two Championships while I'd *lost* one.

He's the kind of guy who will try to get a lever, no matter how small, on the other driver. He'll make out he's hard done by, and there is, unfortunately, some mileage in causing conflict within a team. He's a great one for getting people on his side. He made judgements about me which were inconsistent and at times grossly wrong.

But then he had to do that to justify his position. He was twice world champion, No 1 at Williams, and his status was being undermined because I was quicker and winning more races. So he made up explanations for this instead of accepting that on the day I'd perhaps done a better job. He simply couldn't come to terms with it.

At this level you have to accept that you are dealing with the very best and that on some circuits the order changes. I have no problem accepting that sometimes Nelson, Alain, Ayrton, Gerhard Berger or Michele Alboreto will be quicker than me. If you're beaten, you look for the reason; you don't knock the other guy.

For all his yapping to other people, Nelson rarely said anything to me. There was very little conversation at all between us, even on a professional basis. But then we have very little in common. My lifestyle and his couldn't be further apart. I'm down to earth, and can't be bothered with garbage. He was the one with the problem in our team.

The duel exceeded all expectations. Even the qualifying sessions were taken over by the Williams cars: Mansell's red 5 against Piquet's white 6. Both drivers went off in

*the ferocious contest for pole, but ultimately the honour
was the Brazilian's – by seven-hundredths of a second.*

It was down to the two of us and we were both going
for it. I'm sure it was good value for the spectators. But
I didn't think it was a foregone conclusion that the
race would be between us as well. Formula One is too
complicated; there are too many possibilities, too many
things that can go wrong. As it turned out, it *was*
between the two of us again. Frank's only instruction
was: 'Don't take each other off.'

Nelson, who likes fast tracks of course, got away well
and began to build up a useful lead. At that stage I
couldn't really do anything about it because I was getting a lot of vibration – so much so that it was giving
me blurred vision. I'd lost a wheel balance. When I
changed tyres the difference was enormous. With thirty
laps left I was 28 seconds behind. Just as at Brands the
year before, no one else could touch us.

It was a big gap to contend with, but I began to pull
back and I felt that if I could sustain it I had a chance.
I had to push myself to have a hope of winning, but at
the same time I had to make sure I didn't consume all
my fuel too soon. Everything had to be judged perfectly.

*As the deficit was reduced, so too was the Silverstone
lap record. Repeatedly. Gradually the 100,000 crowd
realised that the Briton wasn't charging in vain. Another
stupendous victory could be at hand. Rosanne, expect-
ing their third child, could watch no more. 'I thought
I was going to have the baby there and then,' she says.*

When I knew I was able to catch him I then had to
work out where and when to overtake him. With three
laps to go I was close behind, but I was happy to wait.
Through Copse and Maggotts and Becketts I made sure
I filled his mirrors: just to let him know I was there,
perhaps to unnerve him a little and keep him guessing.

As we came out of Chapel into Hangar Straight I knew this was my opportunity. I tucked in behind him and then just pulled a little to the right. I had no intention of going yet, it was just a feint. Piquet covered the move. As he did I made a more exaggerated move to the left. All the time I was watching his hands and his head. Even at 180 mph and 190 mph you have to do that to read the next move.

When I went left I saw his hands and head come way over too. His mirror was blocked out. That was the move I wanted. He would be committed and leave a gap to his right. He'd been fooled by the second feint and I switched instantly to the right. He made a desperate attempt to come across again but I was inside him and squeezed through at Stowe. The crowd was erupting all round the circuit. They roared me along those final two laps.

My worry then was the fuel. I didn't need to charge away. I just had to stay ahead. According to my read-out I had nothing as I came towards the line, and in fact, I ran out of fuel on my slowing-down lap. It was that close. By then there were thousands of spectators on the track. I was engulfed, picked up and thrown about a bit, but it was all good humoured. I'd never seen anything like it on a British track.

I got on to the back of a police bike, stopped at the point where I'd taken the lead, and kissed the ground. I know it seems a bit daft now, doing a Pope John Paul, but it illustrates what an emotional day it was for me and also, I think, for the fans. It had seemed impossible, but it was even better than 1986. It was the greatest moment of my career.

Emotion and patriotism can warp judgement and distort perspective, but by any barometer that was one of the great days of British sport. It was a chase and kill of Chataway proportions, a blitz reminiscent of Botham

*in 1981. As a head-to-head confrontation it produced
drama and spectacle comparable with the Watson—
Nicklaus classic at Turnberry in 1977, or the Coe–
Ovett showdown in Moscow, 1980.*

*It is worth considering also that Mansell achieved
this wondrous feat despite having been served with a
writ on the Saturday afternoon. He was being sued for
1.2 million dollars by his former manager.*

*By Sunday evening Silverstone's stands were empty
and silent, the queues of traffic inching towards the exit.
Mansell sat in a fold-up garden chair by the infield
caravan that had been the family home all weekend.
The Mansells were joined by a small group of relatives
and friends. A few fans shook him by the hand or asked
for autographs; most never realised he was there. The
national hero was precisely what he said he was: a
down-to-earth sort of bloke.*

*No one else had finished the British Grand Prix on
the same lap as Mansell and Piquet, but Senna's third
place kept him at the top of the Championship, 1 point
ahead of the Williams pair. Prost was a further 4 points
adrift as the scene switched to Hockenheim and the
German Grand Prix. Mansell was on a high, and stayed
there with pole.*

Again there were only two of us genuinely contesting
the race, but this time the man I had to go for was
Prost. Piquet and the rest were way off the pace. Then,
after twenty-five laps, my engine died as I came into the
stadium. I was out. It was Alain's. But four laps from
the end his alternator belt went and he, too, had to
park. Nelson was handed his first win of the season on
a plate.

*After five runner-up places from seven previous races,
that win hoisted Piquet to the head of the table. He led
Senna by 4 points, Mansell by 9 and Prost by 13. On
the weekend of the Hungarian Grand Prix, the Brazilian*

claimed still more cause for celebration. It was
announced that he would be leaving Williams at the
end of the season to join Lotus. Piquet said his relation-
ship with Mansell had been 'war'.

I obviously wasn't sorry to be seeing the back of him,
but I knew from that moment that the Championship
odds would be against me. I'd heard that we could be
losing Honda engines at the end of the year, and Piquet
was only too happy to confirm the story. He, of course,
would still have Honda engines at Lotus. It was logical
that they wouldn't give preferential treatment to someone who wouldn't have their engines the following
season. That wouldn't have made commercial sense.

He boasted that he'd pulled off the best deal of his
life. He said he'd screwed me, screwed Williams and
screwed Senna. It was the sort of statement you'd expect
of him and, unfortunately, it seemed to be true. I feared
the worst. Senna was already expected to join McLaren,
but Lotus stole his thunder by naming their new driver
before he could announce anything.

Piquet still had actually to beat me on the track,
though, and I had no intention of standing aside while
he picked up his third World Championship. Just as at
Monaco, I put in a near perfect lap to take pole. The
race, too, went much as Monaco had. This time, in fact,
I was just over five laps – or about 13 miles – from the
end. There had been no problem, no hint of trouble at
all.

What happened next is still a mystery to me. The
wheel retaining nut popped off my right rear and the
wheel tilted. I snaked for a while until I had to stop.
The car lost its drive and couldn't go any further, not
even back to the pits. I'd had a few setbacks, but this
was too ridiculous for words. I got out of the car and
sat on the barrier feeling totally dejected. It didn't seem

real. Piquet went through to pick up another 9 points and was 18 ahead of me in the Championship.

And the wheel nut? Williams said they had allowed a little too much 'play' and as a consequence it had worked itself loose. In future they would ensure a tighter fit.

If I wasn't feeling too good then, I was feeling even worse when I arrived at the Osterreichring for the first practice the following Friday morning. I'd had a wisdom tooth taken out the day before. It had been giving me trouble for a while and that week an abscess had developed. I went to see a doctor-dentist – not uncommon in Austria – who burst the abscess but then said he'd take out the tooth. He froze my mouth, and the best part of an hour later had extracted it. I had no choice in the matter. He made me a gumshield for driving and gave me medication all weekend, but it was agony. I hardly slept the first night and every bump on the track was like a punch in the jaw.

At least I didn't have the scare that Stefan Johansson had that Friday. He ran into a stray deer at 150 mph. He was lucky he wasn't killed. Obviously the woods weren't swept thoroughly enough. The Austrian Grand Prix was dropped from the 1988 calendar, both because of that incident and because of the start-line accidents.

The first accident happened when Martin Brundle's Zakspeed went out of control going up the hill. Frankly, I don't think it should have been stopped then. At the restart I slipped the clutch going into second gear and for four or five seconds I had no drive. Several cars got by, but one or two inexperienced drivers didn't do so well and a pile-up was inevitable. Fortunately no one was hurt.

Patrick wanted me to use the spare car for the third attempt, but I was happy I hadn't burnt the clutch and I wanted to use the car I knew. Nelson and I were on the front row but I decided I would nurse the clutch for the early part of the race. Once I was satisfied all was well I moved up from fourth place and took the lead from Nelson before half-distance.

It went to plan and I had a convincing win in my hundredth Grand Prix – on the track where I had had my very first race seven years earlier. It was also Chloe's fifth birthday. I forgot my toothache – only to get a headache. As we were driven back to the pits for the presentation, I hit my head on an overhanging girder. I had a bump the size of a duck egg.

The win could not make up for what had happened in Hungary, though. You can never make up for a race that is gone, just as a golfer can never make up for a shot dropped to par, no matter how many birdies he makes. Piquet had collected another 6 points and was still 15 ahead of me.

At Monza everything we knew by now to be true was made official. Honda would part company with Williams, link up with McLaren and retain Lotus. Senna would join McLaren in place of Johansson. At an extraordinarily icy press conference Honda rambled on about 'new challenges'. Williams confirmed they would switch to normally aspirated Judd engines for 1988.

Nelson and I were on the front row again for that Italian Grand Prix, but all weekend I knew I was up against it. He had a car fitted with the new active ride suspension and there's no question that that gave him an advantage. Above all, though, I just didn't have the straight-line speed. Only one thing can explain that – the engine behind you.

There was no way I was going to give it up as a lost cause. I'm no quitter – it's not in my character. I was determined to give it all I could, and I was in second place, giving Nelson a hard time, when my log temperature suddenly went up and I lost 90–100 bhp. There was nothing I could do but stick around for some points. I was third, which wouldn't have been so bad if Senna, having gone into the lead, had held it. But he went off and by the time he was back Piquet had another win presented to him – his third inherited win of the season.

Patrick admitted I was down on power but maintained that there was nothing wrong with the car. It was only later that the team found a suspension rod measured five-eighths of an inch longer than it should have, which had caused the crossweight problem. That can cost you half a second to a full second a lap. In the meantime Piquet was 20 points ahead of me, and Senna 6 points in front.

After Monza I tested my own active ride car in preparation for Portugal. Over the course of the weekend in Estoril I had to decide whether to go with the new car, which was certainly quicker on full tanks, or stay with my regular car. I went for the active.

Again I was second on the grid, but this time behind Gerhard Berger's Ferrari. Prost was third fastest, Piquet fourth and Senna fifth. We had another restart after an accident and both times I was away well. Berger went through but I began to pull him back and was happy with the situation. I was judging it well, pacing it nicely.

Suddenly, with no warning, the car just died on me. I tried everything to get some life out of the engine, but nothing. Not a peep. Thirteen laps gone and I was out of the race. When they'd got the car back to the pits and it had cooled down, it started up again. Another great mystery. Engines were Honda's business, so we couldn't touch them. You can try, but you get nowhere.

Into the last quarter of the Championship Mansell's prospects seemed as dead as that engine. Piquet's third place lifted him to 67 points, Senna had 49 and Mansell 43. Prost, assisted by Berger's error, moved up to 40

*with his twenty-eighth Grand Prix win, a career total
that eclipsed Jackie Stewart's all-time record. Mansell
needed nothing less than a run of victories, starting in
Spain the following week.*

My regular car ran well on the Friday. I set the fastest
time and I planned to use it for the race. On the Saturday I couldn't improve but out of nothing Piquet
improved his time by 1.2 seconds. A difference like that
had to be down to the car. I headed for the pits knowing
my active car was ready. I'd try that.

As I came in, however, the red light was switched on,
directing me to the weighing machine but I was going
too fast to drive into the gate and almost ran into a flag
marshal, who had to jump out of the way. When I
stopped and realised that I had missed the gate, I
climbed out of the cockpit, down the nose of the car,
and left it there. I ran down the pit lane to my other
car. I still couldn't get near Piquet's time and I left the
circuit rather than have a row with my team.

I came back to collect a fine for breaking various
weighing procedure rules, and had my Saturday times
scrubbed. I had no argument with that. I was wrong and
I accepted my punishment. It could have been worse: I
could have been out of the race. Yes, I'd been angry,
but then I felt there was a good reason. The point is
that, given equal equipment, I have no problem. That
was all I wanted.

I had a meeting with the Honda chief Yoshitoshi
Sakurai and Frank Williams, and told them I was down
on power. I told them I regretted causing some of the
problems but that I felt Honda had been disloyal to me.
They contributed to my wages, and while they might
have made a settlement payment with the team for
1988, they had made none with me. I had stayed on
with Williams partly because of Honda engines. Now I
was being treated as third in line behind Senna and

Piquet. I was in a no-win situation and that was hard to swallow when so many back home were willing me to win the Championship.

It had got to the stage where I was ready to leave the team because of the way things were going. I told Frank that if it was in the best interests of all parties I would go, but he said he wanted me to stay. I told Sakurai that I was upset with him and with Honda. He said I was a good driver and that although I wouldn't be driving for them the following year, I might be able to the year after that. Some consolation!

Nigel would not have been short of a drive. Benetton, under the stewardship of Peter Collins, were one team taking a keen interest in developments at Williams. Collins confirms: 'I never hid the fact that we would have had him if he'd been available. Frank asked me in Hungary about the possibility of getting Thierry Boutsen from us. I said the only way would be if he released Nigel to us, but he wouldn't have that. My ideal team, in fact, would have been Nigel and Thierry.'

Mansell had not, you might say, enjoyed the ideal overture to the Spanish Grand Prix. And yet he treated the Jerez gallery, as well as millions watching on television, to a virtuoso performance.

I had my team-mate on the first lap, held him off without too much difficulty, opened up a safe gap and basically maintained it for the rest of the race. It wasn't unlike Portugal the previous year; the car was fine and I was never in trouble. There was quite a scrap behind me, though. Piquet had an eventful day, a couple of 'moments', and finished fourth.

With Prost second, Johansson third and Senna fifth the table now read: Piquet 70 points, Mansell 52, Senna 51, Prost 46. One issue already settled was the constructors'

Championship. That was retained by Williams. Three races to go, next stop Mexico City.

I took pole and had the satisfaction of a record fifteenth consecutive place on the front row of the grid, but I had to drive right on the limit to get there. On the first day I had a shunt coming out of the fast right-hander on the start-finish straight and was badly shaken. The second day I had an off when the front suspension folded on a bump. Nobody could accuse me of backing off that weekend, and yet I was ludicrously down on straight-line speed.

Coming out of that last corner I was fastest, yet towards the end of the straight I was down by something like 25 kph. I challenged the team and Honda, but got nowhere. So in warm-up on Sunday morning I set out to prove that my car was slower. I went round with my usual settings and was again down 25 kph. I came in and had it changed to the same settings as Nelson's. In fact I even went a little the other way, so that I should really have been quicker in a straight line. All I got back was 2 or 3 kph. I came in and left no one in any doubt about my feelings. They changed the chip and suddenly I went quicker by 15 kph. I was still slower than Nelson, but it was a considerable improvement and I'd made my point.

That's why, although I love the sport, I hate it as well. I was on the limit and even a bit beyond that weekend. It was the only way I could make up for the deficiences of my engine. I earned that pole the hard way. Berger was second on the grid, Piquet third. My car was too badly damaged to repair after that second shunt and my mechanics did a fantastic job building a kit car overnight.

At the start of the race I got terrible wheelspin. Berger, Boutsen, Piquet and Prost all went past. Then Prost and Piquet got themselves in a tangle. Alain was out but Nelson had a push start and, though he was at the back, he was lucky to be in the race. It was decided that a push start was permissible as he was adjudged to be in a dangerous position. But to my mind he was on the edge of the circuit and there's no question he should have been disqualified.

He was lucky again when they stopped the race after Derek Warwick went off at the last corner. He'd worked up to fourth place but I was 45 seconds clear. From the restart he went ahead and was soon able to get up to second place overall. Twice he cut me off when I tried to take him. So I let him go and stayed out of trouble. I had a comfortable aggregate lead of 26 seconds at the end.

Quite honestly, though, we were both fortunate that day. The race should have gone to Ferrari or Benetton, but they were both forced out of it in the first part of the race.

Senna, like Prost, fell by the wayside in Mexico, reducing the Championship to a purely domestic affair. Piquet, now dropping points, led Mansell by 12 points. In this form the Englishman was capable of winning the last two races, and the world crown into the bargain.

Although our deal with Honda would end after the 1987 season, I had been told by Honda UK that I could, of course, keep my road car, the Legend, and my ATC off-road bike until then. But I returned from Mexico to deal with a letter informing me that Honda wanted them back. I got my personal assistant, Sue Membery, to ring them and tell them their car and bike would be at the end of my drive at two o'clock that afternoon. If they hadn't been collected by four, I'd ring the police and have them take the things away. Honda had them collected. Just goes to show what a cut-throat business this is. They couldn't even wait until the end of the season to get their vehicles back.

There was no point in thinking too much about the Championship. Piquet was still clear favourite. I could only do what I could in Japan and Australia. Unfortunately, I was able to do nothing. I had a big accident on the Friday, and that was the end of my season.

I still don't know why I went into that quick spin and backwards into the tyre barrier. All I know is that something happened, I lost my grip and the car turned on me. I went into that barrier at about 140 mph. The force threw me several feet into the air, back down with a tremendous bang and across the track again. Suggestions that I was trying too hard to beat Nelson's time are nonsense. There was plenty of time to do that.

For a few minutes I was unconscious. When I came round it was only to experience the most severe pain I've ever known. I had X-rays and people were telling me there was nothing broken and nothing seriously wrong with my back. All I knew was that I was in agony.

This was, of course, very much Honda's own race, on their home ground at Suzuka. They started to panic a little at the thought that I might not be fit to race. They put out statements that I would be all right, but I knew I had no chance. Whatever anyone else thought or said, I was going home as soon as I could.

As I lay in that hospital bed all sorts of things were going through my mind. I'd taken a lot, my body had taken a lot. Did I need any more of this? And Rosanne – was it fair to her? I wondered whether I could go on. A battle was going on in my mind. I was woken up in the middle of the night by screams: someone next to me had died. I couldn't be sure how bad I was – perhaps I had internal bleeding. The thoughts went on and on.

The one thing I didn't think too much about was the Championship. That was Nelson's, just as I'd suspected it would be from that weekend in Budapest. I certainly hadn't lost it. You can't lose anything you've not had.

It wasn't like the previous year, when I really was so close to it: within eighteen laps of it. This was different. The disappointment was that I wouldn't be able to go to Australia and play in the Open golf championship there!

All I wanted was to get home and get better. I organised my own air tickets and set off for home the next day. I don't remember too much about the journey because I was on painkillers and drugs, and slept most of the way. I watched the race on television at home and really felt very little.

Nelson Piquet's eyes had been watching a TV screen in the pits at Suzuka as Nigel was lifted out of his car and out of the Championship. 'This was not the way I wanted it to finish,' he said. Piquet finished neither of the last two races (Oh, if only. . .). Victory in both went to Berger's Ferrari. The final table: Piquet 73 points, Mansell 61, Senna 57, Prost 46.

10
One and All

Nelson Piquet may have taken over the title from Alain Prost at the end of 1987, but as a champion and as a man he could never take his place. You have to recognise Alain as the complete racing driver, not only of the current era but probably of all time. It's not that he is so much better than the rest of us in actual driving terms, rather it's his ability to pull the strings and get the maximum out of a team.

Of course you have to be quick and, make no mistake, Alain is quick. He can control the race at whatever pace is required; he is so calculating. What really makes him stand out, though, is what you don't necessarily see on the track. He motivates people, gets mechanics working to their full potential. He understands people, just as he understands machinery – and he certainly knows when to nurse his car.

Everybody learns, everybody improves, and I think Alain would admit that he made some mistakes in his early days at Renault. Now he is experienced and still going from strength to strength. He may well establish a record of wins that will stand for all time. Prost is a man who sets standards both on and off the track. He is a great, dedicated, professional driver, and I can think of nothing to say against him. If I can't win, I don't mind if he does. He is also a gentleman, and I have never had any problems with him. If you do have problems with a great driver, it's your own fault.

Simply from a driving point of view, Piquet is also capable of being very quick. When he applies himself and concentrates on the job he is one of the best in the business. As for Piquet the man, that is an entirely different matter.

Just before the start of the 1988 season he chose to make comments about Ayrton Senna's private life and then, according to that article in the Brazilian edition of *Playboy* magazine, he made offensive remarks about me and about Rosanne. As drivers we can all expect some verbal stick at times and that doesn't bother me, but to sink so low as to say things about another driver's wife is a different matter. I can't begin to work out what goes through the mind of a person like that, and quite frankly, I have no wish to.

On the other hand Senna, as I've said, has matured considerably. That maturity is showing itself both in his driving and in his manner. I think Ayrton perhaps came into Formula One too soon, but now that he has added maturity to his speed – and he is very, very quick – he has undoubtedly become one of the very top drivers in the world today.

Another very quick, aggressive driver – and a good guy – is Gerhard Berger. He, too, is improving with experience. Like Senna, he is likely to be one of the outstanding drivers in the years to come, just as Prost, Piquet and Rosberg have been outstanding in the past few years. They are all quality drivers.

You cannot really compare drivers of different eras. It is obvious that men such as Fangio, Moss, Hill, Clark, Stewart and Lauda were all-time greats and that Prost is at least on a par with them. But standards of performance and fitness in all sports improve so much that you cannot make valid comparisons.

I have to say that I find it difficult to accept Jackie Stewart's suggestion that there is no great difference between the Formula One of his day and the present Formula One. It's one thing having a run round in a Benetton Ford at Oulton Park, and quite another competing with a full field on a Grand Prix circuit, pulling over 4 Gs through the corners, producing modern racing times. Don't get me wrong; I'm sure Jackie would still be quick. But as Jackie knows, getting to within two or three seconds a lap of the pace and getting down to the last tenth of a second are worlds apart.

Remember that previous generations of drivers didn't compete in half as many races as we do now, and I'd say it's far harder to win races consistently these days. Look at the size of the field today: we started the 1988 season trying to qualify with thirty-one cars. Obviously it is much easier and quicker to travel around the world now, but that has merely resulted in a more hectic racing and testing schedule. The workload is much greater in terms of time and effort.

You'll hear marvellous stories about the old days, about the parties, the booze, the birds and the smokes. It would be nice to think it could be the same today, but it's impossible. Sure, there are girls around the scene and there's no harm in looking. There are groupies who go hunting from mechanics upwards. I don't deny that the temptations are there if you feel that way inclined. One or two drivers have been known to be. I'm a married man, with children, and choose to be level-headed.

As for booze and drugs, that would be suicide in Formula One. I can honestly say that while I've been in the sport I've known of no one taking drugs. I don't think any drug could enhance performance at 200 mph. All it would do is impair performance – and that would be crazy.

I don't claim that we are total athletes, but we are certainly sportsmen who have to be fit, very responsible and very positive in what we do. As well as skill and courage, it demands great strength to hold a Formula One car through corners, to withstand the G-loading and to maintain a competitive pace for anything up to two hours. When you see a car bottom out, sparks flying as it bumps along the straight at something like 200 mph, the driver can, for a brief moment, have to endure 18 to 20 Gs.

Training is important. I confess I don't find it easy to put on my trainers and go off on a five-mile run, but I make sure I do as much as I have to. The weight-training, the exercises and the swimming all help, too. But as long as you have a certain level of strength and stamina, there's no better training than actual driving. That's the only way you develop the muscles particular to the demands. Because of the G-loading through corners, for instance, you find you build up the neck muscles, and the wrists and forearms also have to be strong.

A sensible diet is another factor, though again I concede that I have my little weaknesses as far as that's concerned. It's fair to say that I have a sweet tooth: I couldn't live without my puddings. I have been known to have the odd packet of cakes or chocolates tucked in a drawer in my hotel room, although I do, at least, try to make them last the weekend! I prefer good, uncomplicated food: meat and two veg, or just a cheese sandwich with a nice cup of tea. Garlic is definitely out!

When I've had to lose weight, red meat and dairy products have had to go. I find that hard, but for spells I'll do it. No other fats either. Carbohydrates are perfect leading up to a race – for energy and for the muscles. I like pasta and will happily eat lasagne two or three times over a race weekend. On race day all you really eat is a reasonable breakfast. Then you concentrate on taking in as much fluid as you can. You just drink, drink, drink. During a race, particularly in hot places like Rio, you can lose up to half a stone. The temperature outside the cockpit can be 100 degrees; inside it can be 130 or more.

Good preparation is vital. I invest a lot of money
getting expert medical attention, physiotherapy and
training advice. Swift and comfortable travel is equally
important. I have spent a lot of money hiring a Lear jet
this season and it is the best money I have ever spent.
On long-haul flights I go schedule and travel first class.
The fitter and fresher I am when I arrive at the other
end the better I am likely to drive.

I like a big hotel room and plenty of rest. If rooms
aren't so plentiful and I have to share with friends, I
always make sure I have two or three pairs of shoes
next to my bed. If one of my mates starts to snore, I'll
throw a shoe at him. It has amazing results! Mind you,
I haven't gone quite as far as one of my friends. His
room-mate was snoring his head off, so he planted a
big kiss on his lips. The poor guy woke up with a
tremendous fright and didn't dare sleep another wink
all night.

*There can be no more tense, exciting, exhilarating,
uncertain a moment in sport than the start of a Grand
Prix. Twenty-six drivers, strapped into their low, tight
cockpits, select the first of their six gears and wait for
the light to change from red to green. As the thunder
of the engines scales a deafening crescendo, an anxious
hush descends upon the crowd. Suddenly the light is
green, the power and the adrenalin are unleashed. Will
they get away cleanly? Will they get away safely? Will
they get away at all?*

Sitting in the car, on the grid, you get a very strange
feeling. You are in your own little world, completely
divorced from everything outside. All else is alien to
you. The concentration is immense, total. I don't feel
nervous now, but there is sometimes a little apprehen-
sion, although not for one's own safety – you wouldn't
be there if you allowed your mind to work like that.

You're apprehensive if you've had a bit of a problem

with the car and you're wondering if it's going to work
all right when that light turns to green. It might be the
clutch, it might be the engine; whatever it is it can cause
you a headache. That's all you're concerned about –
your equipment. Mistakes are rare; it's the equipment
that matters and that worries you. Your heart starts to
beat a little faster. All you want is for the red light to
become green and for your car to get away from the
line.

*Nigel's dismissive reference to heartbeat is typical of his
breed. For 'a little faster' read up to 200 beats per
minute during the race, and even more when overtaking, the moment of supreme stress. That is three or four
times the normal rate of a fit driver.*

A good driver must have a good car to compete, but
equally a good car must have a good driver to cross the
line first. The relative merits of the car and the driver
will always be debated and I certainly don't underesti-
mate the importance of the car. A car's well-being,
however, is in the hands of the driver. The driver still
directs the team on the development programme, still
has to be capable of pedalling the car round at a very
quick pace, still has to maintain that pace, and must
race for many laps against the best opposition in the
world.

Over the years cars have become stronger, tracks
safer and clothing more protective, and yet I know that
I would still have been involved with racing two or
three decades ago. If you want to go racing, you want
to go racing. But in the past the cars, although they
may have been quick down the straights, were slow
round the corners. They didn't have the technology, the
ground effect, the grip.

Even during my time in Formula One there have
been enormous changes. It moves forward at such an
amazing pace that there are incredible differences every

season. I wouldn't say that safety standards have necessarily kept pace with the car. People try to design their cars to be as safe as possible, but unfortunately racing is, in the final analysis, very dangerous. If the choice is between making the car two seconds a lap quicker and making it a little safer then I can tell you, the winner will be the two seconds a lap.

To get the car on the grid you need massive backing, an incredible team and all-round expertise. It's a company concern, with the driver representing the entire company out there before the public. I've been fortunate at Williams to have had some fantastic guys working with me, from Frank Williams down. My engineer David Brown, and my mechanics Ken, Dickie and Stewart, have been essential to everything I've achieved. These are the people who, behind the scenes, put in the long hours of toil, working on the most minute detail to try to get the car that little bit better. They often slog away late into the night, sometimes even through the night, and are still at the track early the next day.

They also have a taste for fun, and that's just as important. They presented me with a magnificent big birthday cake after a practice session in Hungary, and I was really touched. Then, as I bent to cut it, our transporter driver Ken 'Biggles' Sagar splattered me with a custard pie. They keep your feet on the ground all right. Mechanics are skilled, committed professionals. The test is whether you can trust them with your life; I certainly trust my mechanics with my life.

When you put together the endeavours of all the departments in the various companies in the pit and paddock, the result is a spectacular sporting event. For all the technology and commercialism it is ultimately still a sport because there are twenty-six drivers out there competing, actually racing, trying to win the race. It is a team effort, no question. But it is an individual event. In the race itself, only one man can deliver the goods for the team.

Williams, based at Didcot, Oxfordshire, have a workforce of 110 and a budget of more than £10 million to put Mansell and partner Riccardo Patrese on the grid. Canon have been their major sponsors since 1985 and are contracted through to 1990. Their contribution buys not only prime space on the car and on the drivers' overalls, but also the slot in the official team name.

Three companies form the second tier of Williams' sponsorship. They are Mobil, ICI and Barclay (part of British American Tobacco). Next come Denim, the men's cosmetics company, GE Calma, a division of General Electric, Rover and Goodyear. All are entitled to a presence on the car relative to their funding. It's not all take, though; Williams still find space to support The Save the Children Fund.

Drivers' appearances come with the package. Nigel has personal deals with ICI and Mobil, who have, over the years, become loyal sponsors. Other personal backers include Boss, his clothing suppliers for the past eight years, Patrick Motors and Zeon Watches.

Retainers, prize money and sponsorship deals give the top drivers annual incomes spiralling into the millions. Mansell is a top driver, and makes no apology for his earnings.

There is no question whatsoever in my mind that any driver deserves every penny he can get. I've never looked over my shoulder and said, 'He's getting a million or half a million more than I am.' I've never begrudged anyone anything because I believe a driver is worth as much as he can possibly make. If a driver can get what he demands, even if it's more than I'm getting, I say good luck to him.

It's a sport of glamour and glory and, as has been said, you need both the team and the backing. But at the sharp end there is only one person – the driver – and it's HIS life that is in the balance. Each of us has only one life in this world and I don't think any amount of money can be put on that life. We choose to come into this profession and we are aware of the risks we are taking. I don't dispute that. But neither do I dispute any driver's right to get what he can, while he can.

I take a similar view when it comes to promotional work. I have certain prices and if people are prepared to pay them, fine; if they're not then that's fine, too, because I value my time and would rather not be away from home any longer than I have to be. A lot of work for sponsors entails being part race driver, part diplomat. But a deal is a deal, and I keep my part of it.

Sponsorship is so important now that it can determine a driver's prospects of getting a reasonable chance. Unfortunately, it seems there is much more money available elsewhere in the world than there is in Britain. I believe we still have the talent, but that talent isn't always given a fair crack of the whip. Racing for Britain is a smashing idea, providing funds for our promising drivers. I'd like to think that when I retire I might be able to get involved in taking that support a stage further, directing sponsorship towards the British drivers so that we have a better opportunity of showing the world what we are made of.

Martin Brundle switched from Formula One to Jaguar sports cars because he couldn't get the right team and the right break when he needed it. The Jaguar drive is a good one, but Formula One is the place to be for any talented and ambitious driver, and I believe he is wasted outside Formula One. Ken Tyrrell has had two British drivers this season, Jonathan Palmer and Julian Bailey, and I hope he gets the support he deserves.

I came into Formula One around the same time as Derek Warwick, and it seemed that the press wanted to build up a rivalry between us. We were presented as the two candidates to be Britain's leading driver and perhaps next world champion. We hadn't had a champion since James Hunt; apparently Derek and I were the new contenders. I don't think that sort of talk helped either of us.

But we are both mature drivers, doing a job and, we hope, representing our country in a dignified manner. We're both dedicated professionals, but for both of us our families are of paramount importance.

I have a reasonable friendship with Alain Prost. Again, he is a family man with similar attitudes to mine. I play golf with Alain and enjoy his company.

I deliberately don't get too close to any other driver, though. The deaths of Gilles Villeneuve and Elio de Angelis hit me very hard and made me cautious about developing close friendships. I will not allow myself to be hurt like that again. Nor do I seek popularity; I am what I am. I'm there to work, and that's what I do to the best of my ability.

For all that, I am enjoying Formula One more than ever. That is probably because I have achieved a reasonable level of success. I have had four years with one of the best teams in the business and my outlook on the sport and life in general is much more mature than it was.

Formula One has the glamour and the image, yet it can be a ruthless, dirty business. But then it is very big, very competitive and we are playing for high stakes. In any sporting or financial environment you'll find it's the same. If your face doesn't fit or you upset the wrong person, you could find yourself in a lot of difficulty or even forced into premature retirement.

Improvements can be made in the running of any sport or organisation and Formula One is no exception, but today the sport is extremely well run. You have to take your hat off to Bernie Ecclestone who, as president of the Formula One Constructors' Association, got hold of Formula One and made it what it is today. He may not be the most popular of men, just as some of the directives of FISA, the governing body, have been questioned. But you cannot deny that overall they have done a fine job.

The media, too, have an important role to play, of course. In general the press, television and radio do an excellent job and are essential to the sport. The sponsors want publicity; the media provide it. I, as a sports fan, rely on the media to keep me informed, just as millions of racing fans are able to keep in touch thanks to the newspapers, magazines and TV.

The majority of journalists are very responsible, but unfortunately there is a minority who are interested only in controversial stories and the others get tarred with the same brush. You reach a stage in sport where you become 'newsworthy', and I've had to put up with one or two outrageous stories. The more success you have, the more you are scrutinised. We do have a way in Britain of building up our sportspeople to knock them down again. The media come to regard them as public property and, over the past few years, that has been the hardest part of this business for me. This is where I have to make a stand. I have to be more guarded in what I say and I have to insist there IS a difference between my professional life and my private life.

In the end the people who really matter in Formula One are the public, and the sport is lucky to have fantastic support worldwide. To me personally they have been marvellous. The British fans, in their vocal support and their mail, have encouraged and backed me when I've needed them. They have shown great understanding. I can't praise and thank them enough. And throughout Europe and across the other continents, too, I've received tremendous support. That's what makes it all worthwhile.

11

Family Man, Action Man

Four hundred feet up on Bradda Head, Milner Tower stands as a memorial to nineteenth-century safe manufacturer and benefactor William Milner. Across Port Erin bay, high up at Ballnahowe (Manx for 'place on the hill'), Ballaman ('place of man') is, in its way, a monument to the Nigel Mansell success story. Mansell has made this south-west corner of the Isle of Man his home and his haven. Here he regains his freedom, his zest, his sense of direction. The Mansells moved into Ballaman, their fourth home in the area, at the end of 1987, and there they intend to stay.

It has always been our ambition to build our own house, from scratch, just the way we want it. Now we have realised that ambition. I have never been more content than I am when I am at home now, with my family and friends. You couldn't have a greater contrast than being here and being in the world of Formula One. This is a great help, not only because it gives me the escape, but also because by being here I get the energy and the resources to bounce back into racing.

I think the fact that the island is so sport-oriented has helped us. There always seems to be some sporting event taking place here and this is, of course, the home of the TT motorcycle races. The people are educated in the ways of racing and that makes them both understanding and supportive. There is a strong community feeling, yet they respect other people's rights to privacy. Whatever else the future has in store, this is our home.

Just as Rosanne and I have built our lives together, so we have built this house together. It stands for all her efforts and her heartaches as much as for mine.

The house looks out across the bay, to Bradda Head and beyond. The views are breathtaking. Ballaman is huge and sumptuous. Magnificent paintings hang in the hall, up the stairs and in the lounge. A stained glass window, featuring Mansell's red, white and blue helmet and the Manx coat of arms (the three legs of Man), lights up the staircase. A corridor (scene of impromptu games of football involving Mansell and unsuspecting guests) leads from the 'living quarters' to the recreation and business block. There is a snooker room, an office, indoor swimming pool with sauna, whirlpool and gym.

Below ground is a shooting range; outside is a tennis court. There are plans for stables and a squash court. There is a golf green and, at appropriate distances, par three, four and five tees. Space is no problem: the Mansells' land extends over the hill and down to the sea. The treble garage is, however, becoming congested with golf bags. Parking the BMW, the Rover, the Range Rover, the Metro and the golf cart can be tricky. The Mansells employ a nanny, and three full-time general help/gardeners. They have their own JCB, courtesy of Anthony Bamford. The latest recruits to the family are two trained gun-dogs, springer spaniels Frisbee and Gipsy.

The Mansells' third child, Greg Nigel (named after Greg Norman and Dad), was born on 8 November 1987. Mansell maintains that his children could be brought up in no better part of the world.

The way of life, the environment, the order and discipline here are ideal. The children are truly Manx. Chloe was only a few weeks old when we moved here, and both the boys were born here. They know only the Isle of Man as their home. The schools are excellent. Chloe goes to Buchan School for girls in Castletown, and Leo and Greg will eventually go to King William College.

As they grow up I will encourage them in whatever field they are good at and in whatever profession they go for – except, that is, motor racing. I don't regret my years in the sport – how can I? But I wouldn't like to think of the children coming into it. It is such a volatile, unpredictable, up-and-down business; and on top of it all you have the danger and the anxiety that go with it.

I would be happy for all of them, including Chloe, to become professional golfers. I've already got Chloe and Leo interested in the game and I've organised sets of short clubs. Golf is a fantastic sport that you can take up when you're young and go on playing until you're eighty. The professional game has a great earning potential and provides a tremendous way of life.

My love of golf has increased over the years. In fact, it's fair to say that I adore the game; I find it a great help when things aren't going so well for me on the track. It lifts your spirits, clears your head of all the problems and confusion, and puts you in a better frame of mind to tackle the job the next day.

I've been fortunate enough to have played with some of golf's all-time greats, such as Seve Ballesteros, Bernhard Langer, Lee Trevino, Tony Jacklin, Gary Player and, of course, my pal Greg Norman. You sense in golf, even at the highest level, a true comradeship that you don't really come across in Formula One. Our business is so much more intense and ruthless that the drivers and teams tend to be more fragmented.

Playing with the best players in golf can either raise your game or, if it's not your day, expose your weaknesses. I've generally been fairly lucky, and have learnt an awful lot from those guys. Greg Norman, in particular, has helped me a lot with my game and I feel I am improving all the time. Greg has been an inspiration in every sense.

On the island I play on half a dozen different courses, though I am particularly grateful to my local club, Rowany. I take part in several competitions and now I have my own practice ground I can just go out there any time I want, for a few minutes or a couple of hours, simply hitting golf balls. Like anything else, to improve you have to practise, and I get a terrific charge seeing the benefit of working on one particular shot. After our bad weekend at the 1988 Mexican Grand Prix I dreamt I was five under par in the Australian Open. That didn't half make me feel better!

For a long time I've had the target of playing in the British Open. When I retire I'd like not only to spend more time with the family but to concentrate on my golf, and with any luck get down to scratch and achieve a standard high enough to play in the tournaments.

I like all sports. Over the years I reckon I've played or had a go at about every game and sport there is: tennis, snooker, football, shooting, swimming, cricket, anything. I've been known to ride, and when I was young I was intrigued by karate. To be as good and proficient as I wanted to be took time and effort; I was doing it six days a week. It's not a sport to take lightly – that's how you get hurt. The training of the mind and the body fascinated me. Like anything else I wanted to do it well or not at all. But when my racing became more professional, some of the other sports had to go, and karate was one of them.

If you are playing a sport I see no reason why you shouldn't play to the best of your ability. Being a very competitive person, I much prefer to be on the winning side. But I have developed a satisfaction in just taking part and enjoying it, win, lose or draw. Enjoyment is the most important part. I like to relax listening to music or watching a film, as long as there's plenty of action and a reasonable story. Above all, however, I enjoy just spending time with the family and playing with the children.

Nigel's returns to Ballaman mean some respite for Rosanne. She keeps the house impeccably tidy ('Nigel doesn't like things thrown around') and handles the two roles in her life with equal grace and competence. At home she is patient, efficient and caring. As the wife of a superstar racing driver she remains genuine, down to earth, utterly unspoiled. The calm exterior can bely her sensitivity and willpower. At a race track she never interferes in her husband's work, maintaining a modest low profile. She is no pouting, posing dolly bird but a thoroughly well-adjusted wife and mother.

The bond between Nigel and Rosanne has grown ever stronger. Sitting in their spacious lounge, Rosanne talks about Nigel, their relationship and their family now, some eighteen years after they first went out together. 'Nigel hasn't really changed over the years,' she says. 'He's basically the same person I met: warm, private, says what he thinks. I admire him for that. He's demonstrative and not afraid of showing his feelings.

'He is an excellent father. He has a wonderful relationship with the children. He knows how to handle them far better than I do. I envy him that. He has their respect. He's firm, yet loving. His time is limited but when he can he plays and swims with them. It's been hard when they've stood on the doorstep asking "Why are you going away, Daddy?"

'Chloe has his personality. She is a Leo, as he is, and has a very strong character. She is very competitive. She hates learning; she expects to do everything straight away and do it perfectly. Leo is more reserved, more of a thinker. As for Greg, it's really a little too early to say.

'There have been strains through our marriage, but a strain on us rather than on the relationship. We've *been pulling in the same direction and so have taken the struggles together. If we hadn't had such a strong marriage and relationship, it would have suffered. But we hadn't rushed into marriage, we knew and understood each other.*

'I'm often asked about the obvious temptations for a Grand Prix driver. It's a glamorous scene and some of the prettiest girls in the world are around and they go for the drivers. But it's never worried me. There are many broken marriages around and if we had a weaker marriage it might be a threat. But it isn't.'

On the track there is a constant threat. Nigel and Rosanne accept it and face up to it. Rosanne says: 'We are both realistic about life and we are both fatalists. It is obviously a dangerous sport but there are so many tragedies that can happen in life, to people in normal nine-to-five jobs. You have to think like that or you wouldn't go on. You have to tell yourself that he's going off to work, but then just pray a little that he'll come back in one piece.

'I go to races when I can and, difficult though that is, it's far better being there, knowing what's going on. I wasn't in Japan when he had his bad accident. I was woken up at about five o'clock in the morning to be told about it by the team. All I knew was that he was in hospital, and for another two hours I didn't hear a thing.

'For those two hours I just lay there. They were the longest two hours of my life. Lots of things flashed through my mind. I didn't know how bad he was. The Championship was in sight again and we'd put such a lot into it. It seemed so cruel. But what mattered now was Nigel. When at last I heard he would be all right, I sank with relief.

'I am very nervous at a circuit but I can control my feelings and not show them. It's better still with the children there because they keep me occupied. I take a* good book with me and have learnt over the years when to be there for Nigel to talk to and when to bury myself in my book. At least you're there and you know what he's doing. At home you're always looking at the clock, working out whether he's on the track and wondering what might be happening. I can never settle and can never be away from the house for long in case there's a call.

'We were with Nigel in Hungary when the wheel nut fell off, but on race day we didn't go to the track. We watched on television at the hotel. When that thing flew off I just sat with my hands up to my head. Chloe wanted to know what had happened and when I explained her face was so sad. She and Leo want to know what's going on.

'When Nigel returned, hot, tired and bitterly disappointed, Chloe ran up to him, put her arms round him and said "Never mind, Daddy. You haven't won a trophy today but have these." She presented him with a bunch of dried flowers we'd bought at the market the day before. Things like that help Nigel, bring things into perspective and make you realise what really matters in life. It doesn't matter about a flipping wheel nut and the Championship. He's done his best and he's back in one piece.

'The children have slept through many a race, but obviously there are problems taking them with us. When Leo came along we decided we would have a nanny, because Nigel and I had come this far together and wanted to carry on together. We want the children to have a stable upbringing, so it was a difficult decision. Fortunately we found the ideal nanny in Clare Jones. She's about our age, she's marvellous with the children and she's now one of the family. It means I can still spend time with Nigel and that is important because his can be a very lonely job.

'I have never had any great ambitions as Nigel has,

so I joined him in his struggle to achieve his ambitions. Anyone who says her partner is perfect would be silly, and of course we have our differences. But we can always work things out.

'*I would not, though, ask him to retire. I want him to stop the morning he wakes up and says he doesn't want to race any more. Whenever it happens it will be a relief, with or without the Championship. I'd not be honest if I said anything else. The thought crossed my mind after the accident in Japan. But I think that would not have been the right time.*

'*Selfishly, I would have been prepared to call it a day, but I'm sure he would have regretted it. I don't want him saying "Why did you let me do it?" He's got to retire when it's right for him, and there's got to be no coming back. It's got to be the end.*

'*The Championship is not an obsession with me, but Adelaide was one of the biggest disappointments of my life, let alone Nigel's. It was just devastating. In 1987 the most upsetting part was the fact that Nigel was hurt. So many people wrote to him saying he was morally the champion anyway. That support gives you so much strength.*' (As did the many awards he received from papers and magazines across Europe, and from FISA, all acclaiming him for his skill and commitment. He also had an audience with the Prime Minister.)

Would Rosanne be equally supportive if one of her sons said he wanted to be a racing driver? '*Nigel and I are adamant we would say "No way". We've been through it all once and I don't think we could go through it again. If we knew then what we know now perhaps we wouldn't have gone through it once. When you collect your thoughts and look back you realise you must have been mad. The important thing is not to forget the past.*

'*I look round this house now and feel it's something we have to show after all the years of toil and struggle*

*and heartache. But I can also see the Welsh dresser
Nigel bought me the first year we were married. There
are some of his grandfather's plates there. In one of
the bedrooms we have his grandparents' furniture. The
strong roots and the memories remain. The past mingles
with the present.*

'*I do miss my old friends from the mainland. A good
friend I used to work with and hadn't seen for years
turned up at Silverstone in 1987 with her husband and
little girl. We just sat on a rug in the caravan park and
talked about old times. We've lost friends along the
way, but the ones who are real friends have stayed with
us because they understand us and what we've tried to
achieve.*

'*On the island we have new friends, good friends.
When we're entertaining I enjoy cooking. To relax I
swim with the children, or put on my coat, my hat and
my wellingtons and trudge over the fields to the beach
with the dogs. Sometimes the cats come, too. We may
miss the shopping centres of the mainland but the natural beauty of the island makes up for that.*

'*It's difficult to say how we will spend our retirement,
but this is our dream home. We designed it and built it
from scratch. It's exactly what we worked for. We'll
always have a home on the Isle of Man. This house is
going to be standing for many years and hopefully it
will always be in the Mansell family.*'

The action man in Mansell cannot be long contained.
If he's not out golfing or riding his mountain bike you
might find him hurtling around his land on a Kawasaki
350 motorbike, a form of amusement that could have
cost him his life.

I was out having a bit of fun on the bike just after the
1988 Brazilian Grand Prix. I'd already had a nasty fall
off the thing and this time I was riding along the cliff
top when I ran into a boulder. I was flung off and

collected a few bumps and bruises, but I was thankful it was no worse. The bike went over the edge of the cliff and dropped 350 feet down into the sea.

I suppose a racing driver, by nature, will always have a love of speed, adventure and excitement. He has to have a crazy streak in him. I was once offered the controls of a power boat in Dubai and couldn't resist. The old competitive urge came out and I had the thing out of the water, almost corkscrewing, the whole bit. The owner, an experienced guy with boats, said he'd never seen anything quite like it!

That competitive urge has made Mansell a winner of the annual rally sprint competition for motor sportspeople of various persuasions. The event comprises tests of racing, rallying and car handling skills. Organiser Nick Brittan recalls: 'Nigel went into it totally determined and committed to winning it.' Sometimes the spirit takes him above ground, too.

I always wanted to fly and enjoy everything about aviation. I have had a fixed-wing pilot's licence since 1979 and I also hold a helicopter pilot's licence. I owned a helicopter for a while. I think the great attraction of flying is the freedom it gives you, especially with the helicopter. Just to be able to start in your own back garden, lift, hover and fly off is not only fun but a great time saver.

On one occasion the helicopter was also useful in answering a Mayday call. I was testing at Silverstone and between sessions had to fly down to Staverton, Gloucestershire, to pick up the family. A light aircraft, also going into Staverton, had crash-landed just ahead of us in a cornfield. We were at the scene within a couple of minutes. Fortunately the pilot wasn't too badly hurt, but he had a back injury and we were able to take him off to hospital straight away. We strapped him in and comforted him until we got there.

Some of the most memorable experiences I've had have involved flying. I've been up with the Red Arrows aerobatic team, practising their full range of routines, from their base at RAF Scampton, Lincolnshire; in a Harrier jump jet, from RAF Wittering, Cambridgeshire; and again I flew a Harrier of the Royal Navy, from their base at Yeovilton, Somerset. Those pilots are brilliant. To take control of the Harrier is sensational.

It's a good thing Nigel has such a consuming passion for flying. His diary is crammed with racing, testing and business commitments.

I could be a lot busier still, not only doing commercial work, but television appearances, radio, magazine and newspaper interviews. I have to be selective. Apart from the commercials and endorsement deals, I have, with managing director Peter Wood, built up a car business, Westover Motors. We have showrooms and garages in Bournemouth, Poole and Malvern, and employ 180 people. I get over there when I can and keep a Mercedes on the mainland.

When I get the chance to take a real break we go over to our house in Majorca (a Christmas present to Rosanne) and just enjoy the sun, the swimming and the golf. The Isle of Man can be somewhat damp and windy! During the European racing season Majorca is a very convenient base. Rosanne and the children love the place, we have a Range Rover and a Sunseeker boat there, and it's virtually our second home.

Mansell still finds time in his hectic life for pursuits that are not for personal fun or fortune. He gives his support to several charities, including Save the Children, and cancer and leukaemia research appeals. You don't have to explain to a father of three what it means to a young cancer sufferer to be taken round a circuit by a famous racing driver. Nigel's most unlikely voluntary commit-

ment is by way of thanks to the Isle of Man and its people. He is a part-time Special Constable on the island.

After that frightening first encounter with the police in Long Beach I developed a keen interest in their work. Visiting the Police Academy in Los Angeles and going out on patrol with the guys was a real eye-opener. I suppose getting involved in the police work here was just a natural progression of that interest. They didn't invite me to join, it was all of my own doing. I think they were rather amazed when I asked for an application form. But I was accepted and, without any request from me, they gave me my car number. They made me Special Constable No 5.

I just feel that this is a way I can put a little something back into the community that has been so good to us. Believe me, I am very serious about it. Once you are out there you're no different from any normal full-time policeman. It's a very responsible job and when you're on duty you simply do whatever has to be done. I'm just another copper and that's the nice thing about it. I've had a few surprised looks from people but I hope that everyone now accepts that when I'm on duty I'm Nigel Mansell, married, with three children, from Port Erin, and not Nigel Mansell, racing driver.

When you are out there in uniform, you are at the sharp end and have to deal with every conceivable situation. Whether it's a domestic squabble, a pub brawl or a traffic offence, you have to deal with it. I must admit that I've learnt a lot more about the island since I joined the force. Even a place like this can have its other, less obvious side. My experience as a Special has merely confirmed all I believed about the police. In fact, I have even more respect for them and their work. I would just like to go on serving the force and making my small contribution. That gives me all the satisfaction I seek.

On the business side I'd like to think that there is still plenty of scope for me to expand my interests, especially when I retire from racing. Perhaps I'll maintain my links with the sport in some way. As I've said, I'd like to help raise sponsorship for British drivers. If there were an opportunity of getting involved in the running or ownership of a team, I might well consider it. Some years ago, before I came to the Isle of Man, I got involved with a Formula Ford team but I pulled out of that. A Formula One operation demands massive backing.

But retirement doesn't figure in my immediate plans. I am still very much a racing driver and while that is the case racing will be given No 1 priority. Just the way it always has been.

12

Ferrari Calls

Just as the crash in Japan tested Nigel Mansell's resolve to go on racing, so did the first half of the 1988 season. After being forced out of the action at Rio, Imola and Monaco, he had to suffer the indignity of further retirements in Mexico, Montreal, Detroit and France. Not a single finish in seven races for the man who had contested the Formula One World Championship itself over the previous two seasons. In fact to that date Williams' only finish and point had come courtesy of Riccardo Patrese's sixth place at Monaco.

That mid-summer low happened to coincide with the time when Nigel became free to negotiate a new contract. Williams were anxious to keep a driver established among Formula One's elite, but others were equally keen to lure him away. Benetton Ford were back on Mansell's trail, and so were Ferrari. He would announce his decision before the next race, the British Grand Prix at Silverstone.

I had four offers to choose from and that was difficult enough. But there was a fifth choice I was seriously considering, one which would no doubt have surprised a lot of people. I was genuinely thinking over the possibility of quitting motor racing. That option had so many attractions. We were financially secure, I had proved myself on the track, and I didn't need the hassle and the politics that unfortunately come with the modern Formula One package. Instead I could leave it all behind and go off and play golf.

I had to choose an option where I was going to be happy. That was the essential part of it. I had to be happy with it and so did my family. It had to be the right decision for all of us. I didn't want to quit and then regret it 12 months later, realising I'd denied myself a third go at the Championship. At the same time I wasn't going to continue for the sake of it. I wasn't in Formula One to make up the numbers. I was in there to win; to win races and hopefully one day win the title.

The results over the first seven races of the season spoke for themselves. It was very difficult and disappointing to be in that situation after being a front-runner for two or three years. The regulations hadn't, as we'd hoped, given the normally aspirated cars a reasonable chance. We were not able to compete in terms of power and then we had cooling and handling problems.

When I decided to stay with Williams after '86 and not go to Ferrari I thought it was, at the time, the right thing to do. I signed a new two-year contract to drive not only for Williams but also for Honda. In 1988 I haven't been driving for Honda and everyone can see the consequences. I can't forgive or forget what happened in 1987. We lost Honda and I lost the chance of maintaining my challenge for the Championship.

There comes a time when it is right to end a relationship and I felt it was right to end my relationship with Williams. The team had signed an engine deal with Renault to take effect in 1989, but Patrick Head was not prepared to say he wouldn't continue with the reactive suspension and I didn't want to have anything to do with it.

If I was to go on racing I had to have a change. I needed a new start, fresh motivation. But after four seasons at Williams it was, in many ways, sad to be leaving. They are a professional team and without them I wouldn't have won those 13 races over a two-year period. I have to thank them for that. I made some good friends, especially my mechanics, and I will miss them all.

But now, I believe, is the right time to join Ferrari. This is the opportunity, the challenge, I want. After Marco Piccinini spoke to me and I received a firm offer, I thought about the move hard and long. I discussed it with Rosanne and she was 100 per cent for me switching from Williams to Ferrari. I wanted another crack at the Championship, and Ferrari, I felt, could give me the chance in 1989.

Every small boy dreams of driving for Ferrari. The name is synonymous with Formula One. Ferrari have been there from the start and their name appears at the top of the lists throughout the record books. They have a great history and I am sure they have a great future. I feel happy and privileged to be part of it.

Getting a call from Ferrari is a little like getting a call from the Vatican, and I certainly mean no disrespect when I say that. It's just that Ferrari has such a special place in the sport. Italian fans don't just support Ferrari, they worship Ferrari. The car is unique. It is often said that most drivers have two aims: one is to win the World Championship, the other is to drive for Ferrari at some stage of their careers. I'd like to think I might achieve those two aims simultaneously.

Despite all that was said when I decided to stay at Williams two years ago, I have had a good relationship with Ferrari and I feel that this move was somehow meant to be. It was, in a sense, my destiny. The great thing for me is that they have demonstrated they very much want me. Of course, some people will say that the attraction is the money, but I wouldn't have joined Ferrari or anyone else for any amount of money if I hadn't felt it was the right move to make. I proved that when I turned down my first chance to drive for Ferrari, back in '86.

I'm going from one great team to another, and in 1989 Ferrari just might be better prepared. John Barnard – who showed his great talent as a designer by producing those Championship-winning cars for McLaren in the mid '80s – has been working on the new Ferrari for several months. That extra time to work, develop and refine the car could make vital differences when it comes to the real test, out on the track in the next Championship.

Throughout Ferrari I sense a great determination to be on top again. The sport tends to go in cycles and, just as I thought Williams would be winners again when I signed for them, so I believe Ferrari can lead the way again. From Enzo Ferrari right through the team, and indeed at Fiat, there's a real desire to meet the challenge of the new normally aspirated era. They are ready to take on Honda and Ford.

As always, the job of bringing in the results is ultimately down to the drivers and I reckon our line-up is capable of taking on any other in the game. My new partner, Gerhard Berger, is one of the very best in the business. He's quick, he's brave and he's very ambitious. He's a racer who always gives everything. Our thinking and our attitudes are very much the same. We are both committed competitors and I think Italian fans prefer to watch drivers with our style and our competitiveness.

I've known Gerhard since before he came into Formula One and we have always been good friends. We understand each other and I am sure we will be able to work well together. I am equally sure that he will prove a tough team-mate to beat. I have no illusions about that. He, too, wants to win his first Championship. It's not easy to join a team with a driver as quick as Berger waiting to test himself against you. But we are professionals and I don't think there will be a problem. I believe we will compete in a positive sense, pushing each other and at the same time improving the team's prospects of winning the World Championship.

McLaren had no fears about putting Alain Prost and Ayrton Senna together, just as they had Prost and Niki Lauda alongside each other. They put pressure on each other and that just ensured the points kept rolling in for the team. I think that at Ferrari we will have a combination to compete at that level. There should be some pretty hot racing!

I have already expressed my great admiration for the late Gilles Villeneuve, a driver who captivated the Italians with his dashing style. Ferrari fans remember him and adore him almost like a saint. Gilles drove the No. 27 Ferrari and ever since his tragic death in 1982 the No. 27 has somehow remained his car. It's as if his spirit has stayed with it. When I signed for Ferrari it occurred to me I could have the prospect of driving Gilles' No. 27. Gerhard has been driving the No. 28, while Michele Alboreto, now leaving the team, has had the No. 27. I didn't know that I would have the 27, I just hoped I would. It would be a great thrill and a great honour.

But whatever the number of my red Ferrari, I am delighted to get this opportunity. Motivation is so important in Formula One and this move will certainly enable me to maintain my motivation. I have twice come close to the World Championship and I want another crack at it. With Ferrari I hope to get it and perhaps make it third time lucky. The will is there and the effort will be there. That much I can guarantee.

Nigel confirmed his decision to join Ferrari as the Formula One circus was beginning to pitch its tent at Silverstone, scene of his greatest triumph 12 months earlier. The transporters and the motor homes had trundled up the motorways of France and England from the

Paul Ricard circuit, near Le Castellet. The French Grand Prix had, predictably, gone to McLaren. Prost outpacing and out-fighting his team-mate and only genuine title challenger Senna, to take his fourth win of the season, the thirty-second of his career.

Also predictable, alas, was Mansell's fate. After commanding victories in 1986 and 1987, France '88 joined his sorry catalogue of enforced retirements. This time a rear suspension failure cut short his race. The mood among the British Grand Prix pilgrims reflected Nigel's fortunes. In '86 and '87 they had been expectant, excited and not a little tense. This year there was none of the hype, none of the drum-beating. No-one dared hope for another home success; the Brits would settle for an honourable place in the points. The atmosphere of the bull-fight had given way to the air of a garden fete.

Silverstone's infield village of caravans and tents was growing as the family Mansell arrived at their usual site for the weekend and settled into their motor home. Nigel, having announced and explained his switch to Ferrari, was relieved of the pressures and utterly at ease. Yet, despite the catastrophes of the seven previous races, he was intent on taking a positive attitude towards the weekend and the rest of the season.

I certainly wasn't going to turn myself off for the rest of the year. All right, I'd signed for Ferrari and we'd got nothing to show for our efforts up to that point. But I had nine races left with Williams, I'm a professional racing driver and a proud one at that, and I was determined to get something out of 1988. I had no desire to let down myself, my team or my fans. I felt that if we could get our act together we could still manage reasonable results in Hungary and Spain. With a bit of luck – and we were due a bit – we might even achieve some success on one or two of the faster circuits. We would, at least, have a go.

With the Osterreichring off the '88 calendar, Silverstone was the fastest circuit of all, and realistically we couldn't expect to get too much out of the race. As far as I was concerned the priority was to try to do the distance. That, in itself, would have been something to build on. If we made it to the finish then maybe we might get among the points.

First practice, on the morning of Friday, 8 July, did nothing to foster optimism for Mansell and the Williams camp. The reactive suspension system was again giving him an uneasy ride – the team diagnosed the problem as air entering the hydraulics – and twice, through Stowe and Club, he had scares as he struggled to control his wickedly twitching car. In the afternoon's qualifying session he completed only three laps before going over the kerb and onto the grass at Copse. He was 13th on the grid. Team-mate Patrese didn't venture out until the rain was starting to fall and he couldn't even make the provisional grid.

That was not a good day for us. I'd had three nasty moments at 160 to 170 mph and that is not a pleasant feeling. The car went straight on at Copse and there was nothing I could do about it. When you leave the circuit at any speed it does not do morale any good. At Silverstone, the possible consequences are unthinkable. It gives you a very uncomfortable feeling when you have no confidence in your car. You should be at one with the car, not trying to figure out how it's going to handle and which way it's going to go. The problem was beyond the anticipation of the drivers, and that is not a very satisfying state of affairs. It was the most unpredictable race car I've ever had. Riccardo shared my feelings and we told the team what we felt.

Frank Williams looked on in the garage as his mechanics examined the underneath of Nigel's car. They found some grass, but there was no sign of serious damage. The same couldn't be said of the confidence of his drivers. Williams conceded: 'We have problems with the active ride. It's giving us the run-around. It's not collapsing but handling unpredictably. One moment it wants to understeer, the next it wants to oversteer. It's very difficult to get on top of. We've just got to hope we can learn something for tomorrow. My sympathies are totally with Nigel.'

The reactive system, designed to give a constant ride-height and consequently make the car faster, had had a successful debut at Monza in 1987 and Williams had insisted they should persist with the project. For all the problems that emerged in the first half of the '88 season, the team maintained they were committed to it and could not abandon it. There were problems, but they could be solved.

Events that day – and the continuous pleas of the drivers – caused a sudden about face. Minutes after the session, Patrick Head was on his way to the Williams HQ at Didcot to mobilise his troops for a conversion operation. Mansell's spare car would be equipped with a standard suspension system for the following day's practice. If the switch proved successful, Mansell's race car and Patrese's car would be converted in time for the Sunday race.

As design staff set to work at the factory, a frantic search was on for essential components. Head said: 'We needed front disc springs and eventually managed to find a place that had some. It was a shop in Worcester. That was at five minutes to five and they were closing at five o'clock. So I asked the man to take them home and we picked them up from there. About a dozen guys worked all night. I got an hour and a half's sleep because I had another full day at the track ahead of me.'

Sufficient parts were supplied for the other two cars and, back at the track, work on the spare continued into the morning practice session. Once out on the track, Mansell soon found his rhythm and produced consistent, satisfactory times. He continued to run his revised car through the final qualifying session. The improvement on the grid was two places to eleventh. The improvement on his mind was immeasurable.

The difference was in suddenly having a car that behaved as you expected it to, and that, in turn, made me feel much more comfortable and confident. I was able to go into corners and lean on the car. You couldn't be sure enough to do that in the other. I quickly got used to the normal suspension again after spending the first part of the season in the active.

The team did a fantastic job. They put in an all-nighter to get the spare ready and, straight from the box, without any development or testing, it performed better than the other car and we were able to put on some mileage. It was a terrific effort by everyone concerned. There was still work to be done, things to be improved. But we'd been bold and positive, and were making progress.

The change was paying off already. I always felt it would and it's a pity we couldn't have done it before. But what was done was done. The race was 24 hours away and the team had two more cars to convert. They set to work again and had the job finished at 2 a.m. As a driver you can't do anything but respond to effort and dedication like that. I was determined to do all I could in that race. Especially that race, my home race, and in front of another big crowd. Nobody expected us to come up with another win but I began to feel we might get a good result when I heard the weather forecast. Rain was expected.

The previous wet Grand Prix in Britain had been at Aintree, way back in 1961. Formula One hadn't had a wet race anywhere since the Portuguese Grand Prix at Estoril in April, 1985. Senna won that day while Mansell, despite having started from the pit lane, was fifth. Prost, who shared the front row with Senna, then at Lotus, slithered out of the contest. On Sunday, 10 July, 1988, rain clouds rolled over Silverstone and history made a pretty good effort at repeating itself.

Rain can transform the pattern of a race, the performance of a car and the influence of a driver. Rain is a great leveller. The mismatch of turbos v. non-turbos becomes keen competition. Driving ability, judgement and nerve assume new significance. For those bold enough but also talented enough, almost anything is possible, no target out of range. That Sunday morning Mansell looked up to the dark skies . . . and saw his brightest prospects for months.

You'll hear people talking about this driver liking the rain and that driver not liking the rain. It's not a case of *liking* it but being able to take advantage of it, knowing how to deal with it, where to make your move and where not to.

What I don't like is a wet-dry situation. That can be far more dangerous than out-and-out wet conditions because it is so unpredictable. Silverstone that day was wet and I knew that for me it was the best thing that could have happened. We really did have a chance of getting a result at last.

Starting from eleventh place on the grid, I was obviously going to have a big problem with spray. That's the great advantage of being at the front of the grid. If you can get away first you have a clear track and clear vision. Everybody behind you has to contend with the

walls of water. From my midfield starting position I
needed to make progress as quickly, and as safely, as
possible. When you're driving blind, that's not easy.

*Ahead of Mansell the grid placings were: 1. Berger
(Ferrari); 2. Alboreto (Ferrari); 3. Senna (McLaren);
4. Prost (McLaren); 5. Gugelmin (March); 6. Capelli
(March); 7. Piquet (Lotus); 8. Nannini (Benetton); 9.
Warwick (Arrows); 10. Nakajima (Lotus).*

Silverstone had suited the Ferraris in qualifying.
Berger and Alboreto had been able to sustain the power
around this super-fast circuit and, for the first time in
the 1988 Championship, keep McLaren off the front
row. The McLarens had handling problems, and
Senna's failure to make the first two meant that Mansell's all-time record of 16 consecutive front row places
was intact for at least another year.

Even Ferrari, however, had no faith in their ability
to deny McLaren an eighth race victory. Fuel efficiency
would be a major problem for them. Any charge in the
early part of the race would have to be paid for in the
later stages. Surely it would come down to yet another
Prost-Senna duel, and this time the elements were in
the Brazilian's favour. Prost, unlike Mansell and Senna,
admits he does not have the stomach for the wet. Just
before the start, with the rain persistent rather than
heavy, the British Grand Prix was declared a Wet Race
and the drivers were instructed: rear lights on.

From the line the Ferraris held their advantage but
soon Senna was going by Alboreto and chasing Berger.
Behind them, in the midst of the spray, a ferocious
scrap was already underway. As they crossed the line
at the end of the first lap the order was Berger, Senna,
Alboreto, Gugelmin, Capelli, Nannini, Mansell. The
Englishman, relishing the challenge, had made up four
places. Prost, tormented by uncertainty of mind and
engine, was eleventh and treading water.

The March team had had a magnificent weekend, but it became apparent that the contest for the normally aspirated crown would be between the Benetton Ford of Alessandro Nannini and the Canon Williams Judd of Nigel Mansell. Up ahead, meanwhile, Senna had taken the lead from Berger and lapped the hapless Prost with the same thrust. The order, onto the twentieth lap, was: Senna, Berger, Alboreto, Nannini, Mansell.

Approaching Club, Nannini prepared to take Alboreto, but at the crucial moment Mansell whipped out and beyond the Benetton. Alboreto held on to third spot from Mansell but Nannini, thrown into confusion, spun and lost ground. Two laps later Mansell used the same stretch of road to attack Alboreto and, as the spectators held their breath, he went through.

The romp of Mansell, patently enjoying life on the track again, contrasted with the desperate plodding of Prost. After 25 laps and running sixteenth the Frenchman pulled into the pits, climbed from the cockpit and ended his misery. 'I did not want to take risks,' he said. 'Everyone does what he wants with his car and with his life. I decided to stop and fly back home. It is the privilege of a champion who is ahead of the points. I also might have lost the Championship today. We'll see. . . .'

By this stage of the 65-lap race the rain had eased and a dry line was emerging on the Silverstone tarmac. Mansell and others were beginning to dart around the track in search of the puddles. Dry surface would quickly wear tyres designed for the wet. Water would preserve them. But Mansell had another concern. Overheating had been a problem all season and even in these conditions his temperatures were rising to 100 degrees. Water would also help cool his engine.

On lap 28, as Nigel again dived into the rivers towards Woodcote, Nannini took the opportunity to shoot through the gap and claim third place. The young

Italian attempted to press home his advantage and set
the fastest lap so far. But he pressed too hard and,
despite the warning of a wobble, spun off at Woodcote.
He managed to keep his engine going and rejoin the
track. Mansell, however, was gone and about to turn
on the pace.

Nigel put in the fastest lap and, as Berger faced up
to the reality of his fuel dilemma, the Williams gobbled
up the road between them. The man who came from
behind to win the 1987 British Grand Prix at this circuit
sensed second place was there for the taking. Three
more times he lowered the day's best lap time and then,
on lap 50, took Berger on what had become his happy
hunting ground, the straight from Stowe to Club. The
roar of approval coursed through the stands and along
the soggy banks of the Northamptonshire circuit.

There was little for Ferrari by way of consolation.
Alboreto had gambled on a switch to slicks, only for
the rains to return and force him into another change.
Berger continued to go backwards and, on the final
bend, even lost the point for sixth place as Derek Warwick, Eddie Cheever and Riccardo Patrese all lunged
inside him.

Nigel chipped away at Senna's lead over the closing
laps but this time there was too much ground to make
up. In any case, for him, his team and the crowd, second
place was more than sufficient grounds for celebration.
In the context of this hitherto wretched season, this was
a magnificent triumph.

The last ten laps were agony for the Williams camp.
They'd had only one finish until then and here they
were, on the verge of the best result of any non-turbo
car thus far. The tension was eased by Mansell himself,
who was revelling in the drama so much that he was
cracking jokes over the radio. As he came through
Woodcote for the sixty-fifth and last time, he took one
hand off the wheel and waved to an appreciative gallery.

His team greeted his safe arrival at the finishing line with an explosion of relief.

Mansell and Senna, so often adversaries over the past years, exchanged handshakes, congratulations and smiles. Both had immense cause for satisfaction. Senna had his fourth win of the season and was now only six points behind Prost in the Championship: Nigel had reminded the world of his capabilities with a typical drive of controlled aggression.

Up on the podium the Englishman and the Brazilian resumed good natured hostilities with champagne spray, and eventually the Brazilian capitulated. It may have been Senna's victory, but this was Mansell's stage. He stood alone to receive another ovation from the crowd and threw his cap towards the forest of outstretched arms.

Italian fans watching at home on television doubtless found a little compensation for Ferrari's disappointing show in the cavalier performance of their new signing. Ferrari chief Marco Piccinini was suitably impressed, he said: 'I am pleased for Nigel, and also a little for us.'

It's amazing how the fans can lift you. They have been fantastic to me over the years and I was so disappointed for them when things were looking pretty grim again in practice. But then we made the suspension conversion, the good old English weather came to our assistance and people power carried us to another great result. There really is nothing like driving in front of your home crowd and that second place gave me a total of 33 points from the last four races on British soil.

The way things were going I felt I was going to win it. I thought something *had* to go wrong for Ayrton. Mind you, I might have had a chance if I hadn't been held up behind that group for so long early in the race. The trouble was, of course, that there was so much spray I couldn't just charge through at will. I had to be sensible, pick my moment and then make sure I got it right.

Visibility was so bad I couldn't see anything in the traffic. The water itself was bad enough coming up into your face and your visor, but at one point a small lump of rubber was thrown up from a tyre into my face. I had to drop back out of the spray, clean the stuff away and reassess the situation: where to attack and how to attack. Fortunately I was able to get it right and eventually I got through.

It's not easy in those conditions. People may criticise Alain for what he did and his words of explanation afterwards may have sounded a little defeatist. But on the other hand, maybe the decision he took was the hard one, the brave one. Remember, he had two World Championships to his credit already. Your perspective is bound to be affected when you have achieved so much. For him the motivation couldn't be the same. He was not prepared to take the risks and he was big enough to say so.

For me the rain was a God-send. I'd say that result was about 80 per cent down to the conditions, 20 per cent to the change of the suspension. It was good just to be able to compete again, to actually *race* again. Despite the visibility – or lack of it – I thoroughly enjoyed myself. In fact I was joking to the team that I couldn't see a thing. That's how good it was to be up there with the front-runners again instead of limping along to another retirement.

The events of that July weekend at Silverstone served to encapsulate the entire career of Nigel Mansell. Out of the traumas and frustrations came the opportunity, and the man responded. He defied the odds and expectations to win the admiration of rivals and on-lookers alike with his vigour and style. Throughout his racing

life he has had to combat prejudice and move moun-
tains. Now he stands up among the peaks, one of For-
mula One's exalted few.

The World Championship remains an elusive target
yet does not haunt him. The pleasure he seeks from the
sport is the pleasure he discovered in the rain of that
British Grand Prix. He was like a kid with a long lost
favourite toy. It is a pleasure he shares with the people.
He drives with his heart as well as his head. He is an
entertainer, not merely a pedlar of results.

That race demonstrated to me yet again that there is
nothing quite like the enjoyment and kick you get from
driving well. It lifts the spirits and re-charges the batter-
ies. The thrill of racing is why I do it. At the 1988
British Grand Prix I was able to experience that thrill
again.

The reactions of the fans made it all the more enjoyable and satisfying. I've been lucky enough to develop
such a good relationship with racing fans, particularly
in Britain, of course, and hopefully I'll develop a special
relationship with Ferrari fans. But I am very much a
Briton and hopefully nothing will affect my relationship
with the British fans.

Moving to Ferrari is an exciting new challenge for
me and I'm sure British fans can appreciate that. I feel
we have so much to look back on with pride and, given
a bit of luck, we could have so much more to look
forward to. There's a lot more driving in me yet. Hopefully, there are a lot more wins, too.

13

Dream Debut

Nigel Mansell had wintered well. Ahead of him now
was a new chapter in his life, new horizons, new motiv-
ations. He wasn't sorry to see the back of 1988. It
had been a season of gross disappointment and almost
totally futile endeavour. No-one could compete with
the turbo-charged Marlboro McLaren Hondas. They
won a record 15 of the 16 races. Their only failure was
at Monza, where Ayrton Senna tangled with Jean-Louis
Schlesser – replacing a sick Nigel in the Williams – and
left the road clear for Gerhard Berger and Michele
Alboreto to give Ferrari a one-two even the most fanati-
cal tifosi didn't dare to hope for. Senna, however, went
on to win his first World Championship, mopping up
eight race victories and 13 pole positions along the way.

A severe bout of chicken pox, which put Nigel out
of the Belgian Grand Prix as well as the Italian, was
by no means his only setback. The normally aspirated
Canon Williams Judd had reliability problems for much
of the year and turbo boost was always going to prove
the lethal weapon. Mansell, the Championship challenger of 1986 and 1987, winner of 13 races over a
glorious two-year period, was permitted just two
finishes in 1988.

And yet, on both those occasions the old verve,
instincts and commitment were as evident as they'd
always been. He was second behind Senna in a wet
British Grand Prix at Silverstone, and second behind
Prost in the Spanish Grand Prix at the snaking Jerez
circuit. He was able to demonstrate his competitive zeal

*on a similar track in Hungary before the chicken pox
drained his strength, and in Portugal until he was forced
out evading a back-marker.*

*His final race for Williams ended when his failing
brakes could keep him on the Adelaide street circuit no
longer. The fortunes of a season were encapsulated in
that one moment. But the sporting battles would go on.
Body and soul would be lifted again. The No. 27 Ferrari
was awaiting him. So, too, was the first tee at the
Royal Sydney Golf Club. Nigel was about to fulfil one
ambition by competing in the Australian Open Championship.*

That was an amazing experience. It was enjoyable, but
also nerve-racking. People talk about the pressures in
motor racing, but I never feel them. In golf you are
talking REAL pressures. I tell you, that's where the
pressures get to you. On the first day I finished with a
birdie for a five-over-par 77. That was a great feeling.
On the second day my game didn't go so well. I shot
an 86 and missed the cut.

Still, I'd taken part in an incredible event and certainly didn't regret it. I had learned a lot, not only about
golf but about sport and life in general. To compete
and be successful at this level you have to prepare thoroughly, you have to be willing to put in the hard work
and practice. I realised I had to change my golf swing
and I was determined to put that right.

My prime concern, however, was to be properly prepared physically and mentally for the 1989 Grand Prix
season. The 1988 season had obviously been very disappointing. In fact, it was the pits for me. The regulations
didn't give us or any of the normally aspirated runners
a chance. The whole thing was a joke. I take nothing
away from McLaren or Honda. They did a fantastic
job. But the only team who had a realistic hope of
competing with them were Ferrari.

On some of the slower, twisty circuits, we thought we might at least get a shot at them. I was genuinely optimistic in Spain because our car looked good through those corners. But every time I got close to Alain and threatened him, he was able to push the boost button and open up a safe gap again. There was simply nothing I could do to combat that. It was Alain's race and I had to settle for second place.

I was hopeful in Hungary, too. I'd gone down with chicken pox but didn't want to miss the race. Here was a rare chance for us and I didn't want to let down anyone. Bad though I felt, I believed I had to race. I was running second for a while but had to give up before the end. I was just too exhausted to carry on.

That episode taught me an important lesson. By racing when I was clearly too ill to I put myself at unnecessary risk and actually made myself even more ill in the process. I had to miss the following two races. When your life is on the line you can't afford to be anything less than fit and well. I now know that what I did, even with the best possible intentions, was foolish and dangerous. I have promised myself I will never again abuse my body like that.

Fitness and motivation are two of the chief considerations in my racing. I am often asked why I go on when I've won races and made my family secure financially. I go on because I enjoy racing and I have the support of my wife Rosanne. I also have the fitness and the motivation, and while I have I reckon I'll be good for a few more years yet.

For me one of the significant features of the 1988–89 winter was the way in which I was able to train and prepare for the new season. It had taken me a long time to recover from that accident during qualifying for the 1987 Japanese Grand Prix. It affected me not only through the build-up to the 1988 season but also right through the year. I'd gone home after races and just collapsed. I was shot for a couple of days.

Going into the 1989 season I was a different man. The pains had gone and I was able to train the way I wanted to train. I worked hard, really hard. I was lighter and fitter than I had been for the start of many a season. I felt good again.

In every sense I felt refreshed. I'd come to realise there was more to life than getting upset over a motor race. In 1988 I had to cope with the demands of 14 personal sponsors. I never realised how much pressure I was putting myself under. For '89 my only commitment would be to my team and Marlboro. It was as if the shackles had been cut off. I was free and relaxed. I was determined I was going to enjoy my life and my racing.

The motivation came from a belief in my own ability and the very fact that I was going to drive for Ferrari. When you go through a season like '88 your motivation is bound to take a dive and this was just the move I needed. I surprised myself that after so long in Formula One I could find the challenge so exciting.

But then we are talking about the greatest name in motor racing. Win, lose, or merely compete, you're with Ferrari, and that's what matters. Nothing else quite compares with it. I'm lucky in that I've driven for two of the greatest teams in Lotus and Williams. Ferrari, though, are something extra special. McLaren, for instance, may have dominated on the track recently, but they don't carry half the weight of Ferrari.

It was only when I joined Ferrari I realised just HOW special they are. When you walk around the factory you feel the atmosphere, you are aware of the mystique. The history and heritage leap at you from the pictures on the walls. It's an incredible sensation just being at Maranello.

Everything they do is first class. The way they treat you, the way they tend to the finer points. You are made to feel good. I've always loved pasta and Italian food in general, so that was never going to be a problem. At the track we are fed by Luigi, who is absolutely brilliant. The Italians love their food and no-one in the team goes hungry.

The Italians also love children, which I, as a family man, appreciate. When I took my son Leo with me to a test at Fiorano everyone in the team was great with him. They played football with him and generally made a fuss of him. You wouldn't dream of taking your children with you if you were testing with an English team.

When I first went to Ferrari there were moments when I felt a little uncomfortable and out of my depth. It was quite different from anything I'd been used to. The language was obviously a bit of a potential problem and I simply didn't have the time to learn Italian. I have, though, picked up a few words and made the effort to learn some important phrases relating to work.

As a Ferrari driver you have to get used to the attention – incredible attention. Whatever stature you had in the sport before, it is greatly enhanced when you join Ferrari. You are recognised instantly, everywhere. It seems everybody – youngsters and older folk alike – wants to shake you by the hand or pat you on the back or wish you well.

Ferrari is, of course, like the national team of Italy. No other team has a following on this scale. It's great to have the fans on your side, but at the same time you can't expect to have any privacy in Italy. You have to be careful about everything you do and say. Nothing seems to go unnoticed. The media want to know everything that's happening. There are no secrets at Ferrari.

People talk about the pressures and politics at Ferrari, and the Italian temperament, but quite honestly I don't have a problem there. I can control the pressures of driving, over and above that I don't want to know.

Even when we have had seemingly insurmountable problems I haven't allowed the situation to bother me too much. Others can do the overreacting. Being the Englishman, I just stand back and muse. There is never a dull moment at Ferrari. It is certainly different . . . and interesting!

It is also a tough world at Ferrari. None of the people I negotiated with were there when I actually started working for them. It is tough in terms of the workload, too. There is a no more demanding team in Formula One. My diary is crammed with testing engagements. But then that shows they are a very professional team, dedicated to getting the job done, and that is the great thing.

Cesare Fiorio is a determined leader, intent on putting Ferrari on top. John Barnard is a great designer and he shares that ambition. John and his team at Guildford (GTO) have put in a tremendous effort, just as they all have at Maranello. Everyone is pulling together and as a driver there is no greater encouragement than that. It's up to me to do my bit on the track.

I know, though, that if Ferrari hadn't believed in me they wouldn't have signed me. If you are not quick you're in trouble, and that is fair enough. I am not in Formula One to prove anything to anyone. I am here because I enjoy it and have the capability of winning. I trust my record and my driving speaks for itself.

From the start, Mansell's driving was more convincing than any rhetoric. He was instantly quick at Ferrari's Fiorano test track and set the pace in testing at Rio. He admits, however, that he had his problems coming to terms with the seven-speed, semi-automatic gearbox.

The idea is that you can change swiftly through the gears and keep your hands on the steering wheel. You flick a little lever with your right hand to go up, one with your left to go down. As with anything else new, it takes a bit of time and patience getting used to it. Flick the wrong lever and you can have some fun you didn't bargain for, as I can testify. You have to be particularly careful to get it right when you are on opposite lock!

As the first race in Brazil approached we knew we still had a lot of work to do. John's 640 looked superb and the V12 engine sounded magnificent. But McLaren Honda were a lot further down the road in their development programme. They still appeared to be the team to beat. I didn't feel it was realistic for me to be thinking in terms of the Championship in my first season with Ferrari.

And yet I couldn't see '89 being a repeat of '88. We were all normally aspirated now and no-one would be able to push that boost button. It was of paramount importance for the sport to regain some credibility. It had to be seen as a genuine contest again and I firmly believed we had an exciting Formula One Championship in prospect. We undoubtedly had the potential to win races and we weren't too unhappy when McLaren were unable to beat our time in Rio testing.

But in this game it always comes down to one thing: reliability. If you have reliability, you're in business. If you don't have reliability, forget it. We were aware we needed more work on the engine and gearbox and practice for the Brazilian Grand Prix confirmed our fears.

At the end of qualifying on the Saturday we were in the depths of despair. By Sunday lunchtime we were even lower. In the warm-up that morning I'd managed just one complete lap. That's how bad it was. I was resigned to making an early exit from my debut race with Ferrari. In fact, I'd booked out on an early flight. The Italian journalists were giving us 10 laps. 'There they go,' I thought, 'exaggerating again!' We didn't give ourselves any more than five laps. I was even worried about the start and warned Derek Warwick, who was immediately behind me on the grid, that I might have problems getting away.

Mansell was sixth on the grid, Warwick eighth. From the front the order was: Senna, Patrese, Berger, Boutsen, Prost. Senna had a sluggish start and Berger attacked on the inside. The collision put Berger's Ferrari out of the race and Senna's McLaren out of contention. Patrese went clear, pursued by Boutsen, Mansell and Prost.

On lap three the surviving Ferrari was second. Soon it was exceeding the expectations of its driver and even those of the Italian journalists. On lap 16 it was not only still running – it was leading. Mansell attacked Patrese's Williams down the long straight and had the audacity to take it on the outside. A flurry of tyre changes confused the order for a while but never flustered the noble Prancing Horse. Its head was held high, its step was sure. The man holding the reins was in total control.

Twice Mansell regained the lead from Prost with more orthodox manoeuvres on the straight. The temperature was 105 degrees F, the tension in the Ferrari pit unbearable. Rosanne Mansell hid her anxiety behind a smile. Prost, without his clutch, had elected to go on without a second tyre change and knew the Ferrari was beyond reach. Mansell took the flag 7.8 seconds ahead of the McLaren. Victory in his first race for Ferrari and against all logic. It was the stuff of fairytales. Nigel dedicated the success to Enzo Ferrari, who died on August 14, 1988, aged 90.

After a win like that you can talk about the miracle of Ferrari, let alone the mystique. I've been asked if it was a big con-trick and all I can say is that if it was, it had me fooled. It took me a fortnight to believe what had happened. It was such a shock to me that the car kept going. That's what made it so thrilling and, in its way, one of the best wins of my career.

I was amazed when we got through the first few laps. Then I thought to myself, 'I'm going to miss that early flight at this rate.' When I reached half distance it began to dawn on me that I might actually have a chance of making the distance. Then I started thinking of all the problems we'd had that weekend. Surely we couldn't go all the way. It was more like being in a torture chamber than in a racing car. As the end drew closer I nursed the car more and more. I was wondering about the engine, the gearbox, everything. Still it kept going. 'Don't say I'm going to make it, don't say I'm going to win on my debut for Ferrari,' I thought. It's just too much to ask for. But it wasn't.

The gods were with me that day, I willingly concede. But then I have had more than my share of bad luck over the course of my career so I think these things balance themselves out. It was good to get my 14th win and off that No. 13. It was only my third finish in 15 races, but those three finishes had brought me two seconds and a first, so I reckoned that wasn't too bad a record. For the first time I'd started a season with a win. It was a good feeling.

That win was also great for the team. They had worked hard despite so many setbacks and this was a timely lift for all concerned. We had proved that, given reliability, we could be winners and I'd proved I could do what they were paying me to do.

Back in Italy the tifosi were out on the streets, car horns were on full throttle, Ferrari flags painted every town red. At Maranello the church bells rang and the mayor toasted 'this real spiritual son of ours named Nigel Mansell, who has brought us glory with unsurpassed skill and courage.' At Imola there was a rush to snap up the remaining grandstand seats for the San Marino Grand Prix. Even practice was a sell-out.

The crowd gave us a sensational reception at Imola. They really are incredible those fans. The colour, the noise, the atmosphere and the sheer numbers of people made my first race for Ferrari in Italy a very special occasion.

But to put this in true perspective you have to understand that anyone driving for Ferrari would get a great reception. It's the team, the very name of Ferrari that is so magical to the Italians. We saw that again when, that weekend, the circuit was renamed the Enzo and Dino Ferrari Autodrome. As a driver it's good just to be part of the team.

The crowd were naturally hoping for great things but it was obvious McLaren were going to take some holding. They had tested for eight days solid. It must have been the longest test ever. No other team would have the capability of running a test of that magnitude. It would put so much pressure on every member of the team.

There's no question they were responding to what happened in Rio. They didn't have to worry too much, though, because we were having problems. Gerhard was driving for the first part of our test and when I arrived he was tearing his hair out in frustration. He couldn't believe I'd done 61 laps in Rio. Rain didn't help our programme and at the end of the test we were a couple of seconds down on McLaren.

I reckoned we'd still be a second and a half to two seconds slower in qualifying and so it proved. Imola is a renowned power circuit. It is all about hard braking and then acceleration out of the corners. That's why it is such a thirsty circuit. The McLaren Honda's acceleration was vital. From the last corner to our pit, which

was little more than 100 metres, they were 10 to 12
km quicker. That statistic said everything.

The first qualifying session was a bit of a horror story
for me. In Rio we'd had an aerodynamic package that
worked, but here the car was as difficult to handle as
any I'd had. As the track began to dry a little towards
the end Gerhard got provisional pole but I was down
in 22nd place, seven seconds slower. Since my record
in the wet isn't bad there was clearly something wrong
with the car itself. In fact, the front suspension was
solid. The problem was traced to a damper.

Fortunately, the team were able to put it right and
the next day was fine. On my quickest lap I had to pass
five cars and at one point I had to go between two cars.
That was pretty frightening. You just hope the other
guys don't change their line. I was up to third place,
behind Senna and Prost. From the reaction of the crowd
you'd have thought I'd won the race. It was astonishing.
Gerhard had a couple of moments and then spun off at
the end. He was fifth on the grid. It seemed to me that
if we all had reliability McLaren would be one and two,
and we would be three and four, though we would have
tough competition from the Williams.

*As Berger pointed out, it was a rare experience for
him to be outqualified by a team-mate. Much worse,
however, was in store for him in the race. At the end
of the third lap the order was: Senna, Prost, Mansell,
Patrese, Berger, Boutsen. The leaders swept around the
left hand curve, Tamburello, at almost 180 mph but
Berger went straight on, smashing into the concrete
wall, then spinning along it for 200 yards. As the Ferrari
came to rest, it burst into flames. Fire marshals and a
doctor were on the scene within 15 seconds. The blaze
was quickly put out and the Austrian was freed from
his cockpit. Amazingly, he was not seriously injured.
He had a hairline fracture of the shoulder, a broken*

rib, and burns to hands, feet and back caused more by fuel than fire.

Boutsen said part of Berger's front wing had broken away. Later, in hospital in Innsbruck, Berger talked of 'something' snapping. He said he was unable to control the car, took his hands off the steering wheel before it hit the wall and made himself small. He recalled nothing of the fire. By then he was unconscious. Ferrari investigations found no faults in the suspension, electronics, gears or steering.

There's no question that Gerhard was very, very lucky. Without the survival cell and the immediate action of the marshals the consequences could have been very different. The marshals were marvellous. They cannot be praised too highly. Nor can John Barnard. Here was proof of the strength of his car. I wouldn't have got back in my car for the restart if I hadn't had complete faith in John. I went to see Gerhard and was relieved to find he wasn't too bad.

People have told me I was brave to race on, but I don't really look at it like that. I was perplexed and shaken. I was still upset about the whole thing for some time after. But I had a job to do and the team wanted to go on. As I suspected, Senna and Prost went away on their own and I was third until I had to retire with gearbox trouble.

It had been a remarkably eventful start to life with Ferrari. As for the future, who could tell? As I've said, so much comes down to that one magical word — reliability. We had the capability of being competitive and I was still looking ahead to a good Championship, even though I had to retire at Monaco with gearbox trouble.

Beyond '89, I had no idea. I decided, after '88, that I would no longer sign a contract for more than one year. I believe that if you are good enough, you will be offered a good drive. If there is an opportunity that offers a good Championship prospect I would at least like to be in a position to consider it.

But after three races in the '89 season, I was certainly looking no further than Ferrari. We had an excellent, professional team, all wanting to progress and improve. Their aim was to be winners and, whether you spell it out in English or Italian, that's a language I understand.

Even after further retirements in Mexico and Phoenix, where I was on course for good places, I was becoming more and more convinced that I should stay at Ferrari. I had offers from Williams and Benetton and originally intended to make my decision in the second half of the season. But I was happy at Ferrari and that, for me, was the most important consideration. Their offer was certainly a good one. Every driver has his market value and I was fortunate enough to be wanted. Above all, though, I had to be content. I also wanted a team I felt could give me a chance of the Championship in 1990 and Ferrari, I believed, had the potential. Cesare Fiorio had impressed me enormously. He reminds me a bit of Colin Chapman. He is a strong, determined leader, yet he also understands people. After Phoenix I signed a contract for 1990, with an option for '91. I saw no reason to delay my decision any longer and thought it would give the team a vote of confidence.

I went to Canada feeling happy and relaxed. I reckoned we'd go well in the race, particularly if, as expected, it rained. There was a heavy downpour just before the race but as we went round on the parade lap the track was drying. When we approached the grid I dived into the pits to change to slicks. So, too, did Alessandro Nannini in the Benetton. I stormed down the pit-lane and as there was no red light or marshal to stop me, blasted onto the circuit. I assumed the race had started. Nannini did likewise. In fact, the rest of the cars were still on the grid, out of our vision on the other side of the pit wall. We went off BEFORE them. We were black-flagged through no fault of our own. It was a crazy situation. Nannini confirmed there was only a flashing amber light. Both teams protested but the officials threw the rule book at us, stating we had left the pit-lane less than 15 minutes before the start of the race.

That made it a run of five races without a finish, but things were about to change. Before the French Grand Prix, though, came confirmation of changes we'd expected. John Barnard announced he would be leaving Ferrari and Alain Prost told a press conference he would be parting company with McLaren. Again, it was no great surprise when McLaren later named as Alain's replacement my current team-mate Gerhard Berger.

We were less prepared for what happened at the first corner in the race. Mauricio Gugelmin's March took flight but amazingly there were no casualties. I was lucky I had no more than a bang on the head. I must have blacked out for a moment, then gathered my senses and headed back to the pits for the spare car. Mine was in no state to make the re-start.

The 'spare' was, in fact, Gerhard's discarded race car and I was not amused to find it wasn't prepared for action. I had to start from the pit-lane. Nothing, it seemed, was going right. Yet in the race the car ran well and I picked my way through the field to finish second behind Alain. We were back in business.

Our performance at Ricard had showed we were getting closer to the McLarens and we underlined the fact at Silverstone. When Senna spun off it was down to Alain and me. We were well clear of the rest. A puncture ended my hopes of catching Alain but we had the encouragement of another strong second place and we'd again managed to give the British fans something to cheer about. That win left Alain in a strong position for the 1989 Championship but my sights were already

on '90. To round things off, I opened my own Ferrari
dealership near Blandford, Dorset, the following day.
In every respect, Nigel Mansell and Ferrari were looking
ahead to a bright future.

Our optimism was soon reinforced. I had to settle for
third place behind the McLarens at Hockenheim, where
we simply couldn't compete with their power, but in
Hungary it was a different story. It seemed to me the
Hungaroring, with its slow and medium speed corners,
would give us a genuine chance and so it proved. I
spent the second qualifying session concentrating on
preparing the car for the race and although I dropped
down to 12th place on the grid I wasn't too dismayed.

I made a great start, moving up four places straight-
away. Then I had to be patient and gradually work my
way up the queue, taking Prost's McLaren in the process. At two-thirds distance I was up to second, ahead
of me Senna's McLaren. On lap 58, as we came up
behind Stefan Johansson's Onyx, I sensed my opportunity. Senna got himself too close to the backmarker
and as he moved right to overtake I threw my car
sideways to go wider still. I had the extra momentum
to go through and take the lead. It was one of my best
wins, if not THE best, because I had to catch and pass
both McLarens. There's nothing quite like the satisfaction of winning, and winning well.

Appendix

FORMULA ONE RECORD

1980 (Lotus)
Austria
Qualified: 24th
Race: retired
Laps: 40
Reason: engine

Holland
Qualified: 16th
Race: retired
Laps: 15
Reason: brakes/accident

Italy
Did not qualify

1981 (Lotus)
USA Long Beach
Qualified: 7th
Race: retired
Laps: 25
Reason: accident

Brazil
Qualified: 13th
Race: 11th

Argentina
Qualified: 15th
Race: retired

Laps: 3
Reason: engine

San Marino
Entry withdrawn

Belgium
Qualified: 10th
Race: 3rd

Monaco
Qualified: 3rd
Race: retired
Laps: 16
Reason: rear suspension

Spain
Qualified: 11th
Race: 6th

France
Qualified: 13th
Race: 7th

Britain
Did not qualify

Germany
Qualified: 15th
Race: retired
Laps: 12
Reason: fuel leak

Austria
Qualified: 11th
Race: retired
Laps: 23
Reason: engine

Holland
Qualified: 17th but 16th on grid after De Cesaris withdrawn
Race: retired
Laps: 1
Reason: electrics

Italy
Qualified: 12th
Race: retired
Laps: 21
Reason: handling

Canada
Qualified: 5th
Race: retired
Laps: 45
Reason: accident

USA Las Vegas
Qualified: 9th
Race: 4th

Non-championship F1
South Africa
Qualified: 8th
Race: 10th

1982 (Lotus)
South Africa
Qualified: 18th
Race: retired

Laps: 0
Reason: electrics

Brazil
Qualified: 14th
Race: 5th, placed 3rd after two drivers disqualified

USA Long Beach
Qualified: 17th
Race: 7th

San Marino
FOCA boycott

Belgium
Qualified: 7th
Race: retired
Laps: 9
Reason: clutch

Monaco
Qualified: 11th
Race: 4th

USA Detroit
Qualified: 7th
Race: retired
Laps: 44
Reason: engine

Canada
Qualified: 14th
Race: retired
Laps: 1
Reason: accident

Holland
Missed, wrist injury

Britain
Qualified: 23rd
Race: retired
Laps: 9
Reason: handling/driver
discomfort

France
Missed, wrist problem

Germany
Qualified: 17th
Race: 9th

Austria
Qualified: 12th
Race: retired
Laps: 17
Reason: engine

Swiss (Dijon, France)
Qualified: 26th
Race: 8th

Italy
Qualified: 23rd
Race: 7th

USA Las Vegas
Qualified: 21st
Race: retired
Laps: 8
Reason: incident/broken
suspension

1983 (Lotus)
Brazil
Qualified: 22nd
Race: 12th

USA Long Beach
Qualified: 13th
Race: 12th

France
Qualified: 18th
Race: retired
Laps: 6
Reason: driver injury/
handling

San Marino
Qualified: 15th
Race: retired
Laps: 56
Reason: accident/rear wing
failure

Monaco
Qualified: 13th
Race: retired
Laps: 0
Reason: accident

Belgium
Qualified: 19th
Race: retired
Laps: 30
Reason: gearbox

USA Detroit
Qualified: 14th
Race: 6th

Canada
Qualified: 18th
Race: retired
Laps: 43
Reason: handling/tyres

Britain
Qualified: 18th
Race: 4th

Germany
Qualified: 17th
Race: retired
Laps: 1
Reason: engine

Austria
Qualified: 3rd
Race: 5th

Holland
Qualified: 5th
Race: retired
Laps: 26
Reason: spun off

Italy
Qualified: 11th
Race: 8th

Europe (Brands Hatch)
Qualified: 3rd
Race: 3rd

South Africa
Qualified: 7th
Race: running/
not classified
Laps: 68

1984 (Lotus)
Brazil
Qualified: 5th
Race: retired
Laps: 35
Reason: accident

South Africa
Qualified: 3rd
Race: retired
Laps: 1
Reason: turbo inlet duct

Belgium
Qualified: 10th
Race: retired
Laps: 14
Reason: clutch

San Marino
Qualified: 18th
Race: retired
Laps: 2
Reason: brakes/spun off

France
Qualified: 6th
Race: 3rd

Monaco
Qualified: 2nd
Race: retired
Laps: 15
Reason: hit barrier

Canada
Qualified: 7th
Race: 6th

USA Detroit
Qualified: 3rd
Race: retired
Laps: 27
Reason: gearbox

USA Dallas
Qualified: 1st
Race: 6th

Laps: 64
Reason: gearbox but classified

Britain
Qualified: 8th
Race: retired
Laps: 24
Reason: gearbox

Germany
Qualified: 16th
Race: 4th

Austria
Qualified: 8th
Race: retired
Laps: 32
Reason: engine

Holland
Qualified: 12th
Race: 3rd

Italy
Qualified: 7th
Race: retired
Laps: 13
Reason: spun off

Europe (Nurburgring)
Qualified: 8th
Race: retired
Laps: 51
Reason: engine

Portugal
Qualified: 6th
Race: retired
Laps: 52

Reason: lost brake fluid/spun off

1985 (Williams)
Brazil
Qualified: 5th
Race: retired
Laps: 8
Reason: broken exhaust/accident damage

Portugal
Qualified: 9th
Race: 5th, pit-lane start

San Marino
Qualified: 7th
Race: 5th

Monaco
Qualified: 2nd
Race: 7th

Canada
Qualified: 16th
Race: 6th

USA Detroit
Qualified: 2nd
Race: retired
Laps: 26
Reason: accident

France
Did not race, accident in practice

Britain
Qualified: 5th
Race: retired

Laps: 17
Reason: clutch

Germany
Qualified: 10th
Race: 6th

Austria
Qualified: 2nd
Race: retired
Laps: 25
Reason: engine

Holland
Qualified: 7th
Race: 6th

Italy
Qualified: 3rd
Race: retired
Laps: 47
Reason: engine

Belgium
Qualified: 7th
Race: 2nd

Europe (Brands Hatch)
Qualified: 3rd
Race: 1st

South Africa
Qualified: 1st
Race: 1st

Australia
Qualified: 2nd
Race: retired
Laps: 1
Reason: transmission

1986 (Williams)
Brazil
Qualified: 3rd
Race: retired
Laps: 0
Reason: accident

Spain
Qualified: 3rd
Race: 2nd

San Marino
Qualified: 3rd
Race: retired
Laps: 8
Reason: engine

Monaco
Qualified: 2nd
Race: 4th

Belgium
Qualified: 5th
Race: 1st

Canada
Qualified: 1st
Race: 1st

USA Detroit
Qualified: 2nd
Race: 5th

France
Qualified: 2nd
Race: 1st

Britain
Qualified: 2nd
Race: 1st

Germany
Qualified: 6th
Race: 3rd

Hungary
Qualified: 4th
Race: 3rd

Austria
Qualified: 6th
Race: retired
Laps: 32
Reason: driveshaft c/v joint

Italy
Qualified: 3rd
Race: 2nd

Portugal
Qualified: 2nd
Race: 1st

Mexico
Qualified: 3rd
Race: 5th

Australia
Qualified: 1st
Race: retired
Laps: 63
Reason: tyre failure

1987 (Williams)
Brazil
Qualified: 1st
Race: 6th

San Marino
Qualified: 2nd
Race: 1st

Belgium
Qualified: 1st
Race: retired
Laps: 17
Reason: accident damage

Monaco
Qualified: 1st
Race: retired
Laps: 29
Reason: wastegate pipe

USA Detroit
Qualified: 1st
Race: 5th

France
Qualified: 1st
Race: 1st

Britain
Qualified: 2nd
Race: 1st

Germany
Qualified: 1st
Race: retired
Laps: 25
Reason: engine

Hungary
Qualified: 1st
Race: retired
Laps: 70
Reason: loose wheel

Austria
Qualified: 2nd
Race: 1st

Italy
Qualified: 2nd
Race: 3rd

Portugal
Qualified: 2nd
Race: retired
Laps: 13
Reason: electrics/engine cut out

Spain
Qualified: 2nd
Race: 1st

Mexico
Qualified: 1st
Race: 1st

Japan
Crash during practice, unfit to drive

Australia
Unfit to drive

1988 (Williams)
Brazil
Qualified: 2nd
Race: retired
Laps: 18
Reason: overheating

San Marino
Qualified: 11th
Race: retired
Laps: 42
Reason: electrics

Monaco
Qualified: 5th
Race: retired
Laps: 32
Reason: accident

Mexico
Qualified: 14th
Race: retired
Laps: 20
Reason: engine

Canada
Qualified: 9th
Race: retired
Laps: 28
Reason: engine

USA Detroit
Qualified: 6th
Race: retired
Laps: 18
Reason: electrics

France
Qualified: 9th
Race: retired
Laps: 48
Reason: rear suspension

Britain
Qualified: 11th
Race: 2nd

Germany
Qualified: 11th
Race: retired
Laps: 16
Reason: gearbox/accident

Hungary
Qualified: 2nd
Race: retired
Laps: 60
Reason: exhaustion

Belgium
Missed, illness

Italy
Missed, illness

Portugal
Qualified: 6th
Race: retired
Laps: 54
Reason: accident

Spain
Qualified: 3rd
Race: 2nd

Japan
Qualified: 8th
Race: retired
Laps: 24
Reason: accident

Australia
Qualified: 3rd
Race: retired
Laps: 65
Reason: brakes/accident

1989 (Ferrari)
Brazil
Qualified: 6th
Race: 1st

San Marino
Qualified: 3rd
Race: retired
Laps: 23
Reason: gearbox

Monaco
Qualified: 5th
Race: retired
Laps: 30
Reason: gearbox

Mexico
Qualified: 3rd
Race: retired
Laps: 43
Reason: gearbox

USA, Phoenix
Qualified: 4th
Race: retired
Laps: 31
Reason: alternator

Canada
Qualified: 5th
Race: black-flagged
Laps: 0

France
Qualified: 3rd, but started
from pit-lane
Race: 2nd

Britain
Qualified: 3rd
Race: 2nd

Germany
Qualified: 3rd
Race: 3rd

Hungary
Qualified: 12th
Race: 1st

Belgium
Qualified: 6th
Race: 3rd

Index